Growing a Christian Family

RIGHT
from the
START

A New Parent's Guide
to Child Faith Development

Shirley K. M

CPH™
SAINT LOUIS

To my dear family,
who has in many ways made this book possible,
and especially to my parents,
Roland and Hattie Kloha,
whose rootedness in Jesus Christ
has shaped a storehouse
of memories and a legacy of values
and faith to give
to succeeding generations.

Shirley K. Morgenthaler

Unless otherwise noted, the Scripture quotations in this publication are from The Holy Bible: NEW INTERNATIONAL VERSION, © 1973, 1978, 1984 by the International Bible Society. Used by permission of Zondervan Bible Publishers.

Copyright © 1989 Concordia Publishing House
3558 S. Jefferson Avenue, St. Louis, MO 63118-3968
Manufactured in the United States of America

Library of Congress Cataloging-in-Publication Data

Morgenthaler, Shirley K., 1938–
      Right from the start: a new parent's guide to child faith development/ Shirley K. Morgenthaler
        p. cm. — (Good news for families. Growing Christian family series)
        ISBN 0-570-04533-9
        1. Family—Religious life. 2. Parenting–Religious aspects—Christianity. 3. Children—Religious life. 4. Faith. I. Title. II. Series
BV4526.2.M59 1989
248.8'45—dc20
                                        89-33955

2 3 4 5 6 7 8 9 10 11   03 02 01 00 99 98 97 96 95 94

Contents

THE CHILD

CHAPTER ONE

New Parent Jitters

"We're going to have a baby!" The happy news travels across telephone lines to parents and friends. Everyone is ecstatic. For months, maybe years this baby has been wanted and prayed for.

Even if the baby comes at a time you had not planned, you nevertheless accept God's timing as good. You look forward to the baby's coming.

Plans and priorities are adjusted. Suddenly, everything you do and plan revolves around *the due date*. Everything is calculated as B.B. (Before Baby) and A.B. (After Baby). You find yourself caught in a whirl of excitement, planning, and anticipation.

B.B. decisions need to be made: obstetrician or midwife—hospital or home delivery—breast or bottle feeding—delivery preparation classes—cloth or throw-away diapers.

Some A.B. decisions also need to be made: Where will the baby sleep? What about all the furniture and paraphernalia we'll need? Will Mom quit her job or take a leave of absence? How long a leave of absence?

The child inside grows—and begins to kick—to move when Mom moves—to respond to Mom's emotions—to react to sounds—maybe even keeping time with music—to hear your voice when you talk to "it." Is it to "him" or to "her" that you say "I love you" each night, as you also say those words to each other?

Suddenly the big day arrives. You're *parents!* You can hardly contain your pride, joy, nervousness, and overwhelming sense of awe at the miracle of creation of new life. You quickly thank God for a safe delivery and a healthy baby. He's here! She's here!

Can We Really Care for All of Baby's Needs?

Now the rush of new decisions and responsibilities comes even faster than you expected. Is everything really ready? Who will be there to help us for the first days or weeks? What term of endearment or nickname will we use as we rock and cuddle our Frederick Roger Smithson III?

Here it is—your first night at home with the baby—alone—all alone! "How could adding a baby, a third person, make me feel more alone than when there were only two of us? Is this really happening? Why weren't we fully prepared for the changes that this seven-pound bundle of noise and needs is creating in our lives?"

Welcome to the Real World of New-Parent Jitters!

It's a quarter-century ago, but my husband, Bob, and I still vividly remember those first hours, that first *long* night, alone with our new daughter. Was she really asleep? Was she alive? Would we hear her if she woke up? Could we safely go to sleep ourselves? Should we take turns sleeping—"just in case"?

We lay there listening to the quiet. The soft noises were awesome—the peaceful breaths, the gurgling breaths, the little sighs, the funny noises—unfamiliar, strange sounds of a newborn infant sleeping—all normal noises, but how were we to know? "Dear God, keep her safe," I prayed. "Keep me strong," I added. "The job is so big and I feel so small!" At that time I was a classroom teacher—of other people's children. I knew about kids—but not about babies! Kids in the classroom had survived their own parents' inexperience before they ever got to me. Now, this one had to survive me. Help!

New-Parent Jitters

Needless to say, we did survive. So did Diane. But we never completely outgrew those new-parent jitters.

They were repeated twice over the next years as a son, then another daughter were added to our family. The importance of our task and the sense of wonder at God's choice of us as parents never diminished. Each new baby was special. Each time we asked God to give us strength to meet the task which He had entrusted to us.

Now God has charged you with a new task of parenting. He has given both of you the child your love has created. Whether for the first or fifth time, it is an awesome trust. There is no more important task than to train a child.

At first the physical and emotional needs may be overwhelming. New parents are never completely prepared for the 24-hour, full-time demands of parenting an infant. Nor have they learned everything necessary—how to diaper a real, live wriggling baby without pin-pricks; how to hold her so she can burp; how to distinguish between his cry for food and for a diaper change; how to communicate love and security to this new life. Be patient. You will learn all these things with time.

But there's more to parenting than meeting physical needs. What about the child's most important needs, the spiritual ones? What are they? Carrying them out is not an easy task. What do I do? Not do? Unfortunately, some parents don't even ask such questions until several years have passed. And, when they do, they assume the answers are simple and easy. They aren't.

For Christians, meeting our children's spiritual needs is an absolute necessity. Some of us may differ as to how we fulfill those obligations. For example, I want to tell you frankly that I believe in infant baptism. But even if you differ with me on this point, you will find that what I say in this book is applicable and useful for all of us as we strive toward our common goals: (1) to help our children understand that Jesus has redeemed and saved us, and (2) to do what we can to help them grow and remain in that faith. I find that even those who subscribe to infant baptism sometimes differ in their understanding of it.

Nurturing the faith that the Holy Spriit has generated is a continuing responsibility. Some parents take for granted that baptism is a magical process. They may view the rite as an "immunization" that guarantees faith-nurturing for several years. But baptism is really quite different and unique. *Welcome to the Family: For Parents Whose Child Is About to Be Baptized* (CPH, 1989) puts it this way:

"In baptism God *claims* your child and *names* your child. Through water and the Word your child is set aside as belonging to God's family, marked and sealed with the cross of Christ. Through God's grace your child is named an inheritor of all the good gifts the loving Creator God has to give."

Baptism and its meaning in the life of the child and of the child's parents are the foundation for this book. Baptism means being made right, right from the start by the grace of God. It also means that parents have a special relationship with and responsibility for this child of God.

Christ has described that responsibility. He commanded that we bring children to Him, including infants and toddlers. The kingdom of God, He said, belongs to "such as these." Bringing young children to Jesus is a continuous process. We are to "train up" a child. We "let" the child come to Jesus *repeatedly*. We tell the child of Jesus' love *repeatedly*. When Jesus tells the disciples to let the little children come to Him, He is speaking not only of preschoolers but also of infants and toddlers. (The word used for "little children" in Mark 10 includes the idea of "crawlers.") Jesus commands adults to encourage that "coming," because He knows that the faith of these little ones—yours included—can indeed be developed and nurtured. "Of such" is His kingdom. Little children belong there. And it is parents who bring them.

Can We Truly Teach an Infant about Jesus?

How do you bring a little child to Jesus—a child so

9

small who doesn't yet walk—or talk—or even coo? Can it really be done? Yes.

As a child development specialist, I've spent much time puzzling over the spiritual growth of a child. As a Christian, I've tried to identify what God tells us in His Word about the faith of young children. As a parent, I've puzzled over the same issues that trouble all new parents. As a teacher and administrator, I've tried to help new parents understand and support their children's faith development. As a person who grew up in a Christian home, I remember some of the experiences and rituals which supported my own childhood faith. Through it all, I've learned that there are some clear guidelines to follow.

God Has Confidence in You

This child comes to you as a trust from your heavenly Father. God is committing this child to your care and nurture, thereby signaling His assurance that you *can* learn what is needed. You can become the parent God wants. You *are* capable of this new and awesome task.

God Is with You

"But the task is so big and I am so small." Yes, the task *is* big. But, no, you are not so small. God Himself stands beside you to give you the courage and the wisdom to nurture this new soul. He promises to give you the strength equal to the task (1 Cor. 10:13). Just as God cares for you, He will care for this child through you, as He uses you to personalize that care. What a comfort that care from God can be through the long days and busy nights ahead!

Draw on Your Experience

What prior experience, if any, have you had, learning to care for and nurture children? Any younger siblings? Nieces and nephews? Babysitting experiences as a teen?

Enrollment in a child development class in high school or college (providing at least some textbook information about little children)?

Even if your experiences seem minimal, they are valuable, for you will have learned one basic fact: Even infants interact with people around them, learning to love and to trust—two of faith's basics.

Pray and Share Your Faith with Your Child

You are your child's first teacher. You introduce her to Jesus and His love. What happens these first three years in part determines lifelong attitudes and dispositions. You want your child to acquire a prayerful habit and frame of mind—a disposition of praise—of trust—of hope—of confidence in God's promises.

As the child's parents, you engender dispositions and attitudes, along with the diapering and the burping and the cooing. *How* you develop these early attitudes, *how* you contribute to your child's early concept of God, *how* you begin early rituals and expectations is vitally important. Two or three years from now that foundation will be of major importance as you entrust your child to her first Sunday school teacher. That teacher will in turn build upon your foundation.

Don't Be Afraid to Seek Help

All parents can use help in identifying and thinking about the unfolding faith of the new life entrusted to them. Each child is a new life—new physically—new cognitively—new socially, emotionally, and spiritually. This book is designed to help. It will provide an understanding of the experiences and the environment that are needed for your child to grow up in Christ. May the Holy Spirit direct us as we travel through these pages and ideas together.

CHAPTER TWO

So You're Not an Expert

New Parent and New Baby

During the first three years of life the young child develops more rapidly than at any other time. The child's cognitive abilities virtually explode as new tasks are tried and mastered. Social awareness begins with that first act of reaching and responding to the adult who first reaches out to the child. Emotional growth and stability develop as parents meet the child's cries with appropriate and adequate responses. Physical growth is marked and celebrated—the first grasp, the first attempts at sitting alone, the first steps, the ability to run on two wobbly legs.

Spiritual growth likewise takes place—or fails to take place—during these earliest years. It's harder to recognize, and therefore harder to measure. But it happens. In fact, spiritual milestones are interwoven with achievements in the physical, emotional, social, and cognitive areas. Providing the best opportunity for growth as a whole person calls for understanding. The more you know, the more likely you will do what is best for *your* child, that new legacy from the Lord.

We usually come equipped with a degree of common sense and intuition that gets us through the new-parent/new-baby phase with a fair degree of success. But most of us want more than a "fair degree" of achievement. We all would like to give our child the best chance to grow into a confident and competent person.

The Circle of Response

The more you become a student of children—especially of your own child—the more likely you are to respond confidently and competently to each new learning experience or accomplishment. Your responses in turn inspire confidence and competence in your baby. That circle of response enhances the development of new competencies and confidence in both of you and continues to grow. Nothing encourages success like success!

Getting that circle of response started is the challenge. But there is help. God empowers you—in fact, starts the circle. He gives both you and your baby the ability to respond to each other—to encourage each other—to mutually reinforce each other's responses.

Baby Talk

Almost all mothers—fathers, too—reply to their child's early communication with cooing, gurgling, and words of encouragement. All of us can become experts at encouraging the child's responses. How "expert" we become depends in large measure on our recognition of the importance of this type of interaction and also on our confidence to trust our instincts to "do what comes naturally."

Several years ago, I volunteered to babysit for my nephew in order to give my sister—a new, first-time parent—a much-needed break. Three-month-old Jason was to spend an entire Saturday with me. At the appointed time, he came—complete with diapers, food, infant seat, and extra clothes—everything a baby could want—except, of course, for the loving, watchful adult. That was *my* job for the day. I had looked forward to it, not only for the opportunity to enjoy Jason and his accomplishments, but also because this was my chance to observe first-hand all that I was learning about child development in my formal study. I knew about bonding, socialization, early communication, about all the cognitive tasks in which a three-month-old might be expected to have an interest. Now I could learn about Jason and see how he measured up to the classroom theory I was studying.

We had a great day. I fed Jason, diapered him, encouraged him to reach for things, and tracked his auditory and visual responses. But the talking was the best part. Jason and I just sat gurgling, babbling, and cooing for as long as he remained interested—up to 10 or 15 minutes at a time. What fun!

He really was an infant expert at responding to the sounds and coos I made. I started by imitating his sounds, then gradually changed my responses to add variety—dissonance—to our interchange. If he said "ah," I said "ah, ah." If he said "oo," I said "ooooo," and later "ooo-ah." His attempts at imitating me as I imitated him kept my interest in our verbal play going. (How I wished later that I had taped our "conversation" so that I could have used it in one of my course lectures!)

During one of our especially productive interludes of verbal play, my teenage son Dan walked in. If I had been a new mother, I would probably have stopped my conversation with Jason and talked to this new person on the scene. Other adults often inhibit our interchanges with young children. But as an experienced parent and a student of child development, I ignored Dan. I kept right on cooing and babbling and talking to Jason as a real person. Dan stopped and listened. He shook his head. "You're crazy, Mom," he said, as only a 16-year-old can. "You know Jason can't understand a word you're saying. He's only a baby. You sound ridiculous talking to him like that!"

I stopped. Fifteen years earlier I could not have defended my behavior. In fact, I might not have allowed another adult to catch me talking to a baby! But the confidence I had acquired through parenting my own children—and later through studying child development—let me continue our conversation and make a fool of myself in my son's eyes.

At his question, however, I stopped because I had an answer. I could explain about responding to the child and encouraging responses from the child. I could talk about building a conversational format, a sense of turntaking. I could talk about building "interactional expectations" between the child and a loving, interested adult. All important-sounding stuff. Dan shook his head, shrugged his shoulders, and continued on his way. "Well," I thought, "so much for teaching a teenager anything about child development."

Several hours later I was busy with some mundane Saturday chores. I asked my son to pick up Jason and keep him entertained for a while as I finished my task. A few minutes later I came back into the room to hear Dan talking and cooing to Jason—and to hear Jason respond. Dan had listened! And because I had given him important-sounding explanations for what really happens as an adult and a child interact, he, too, continued his conversation with Jason as he became aware of my presence. His new knowledge gave him permission to do what he had earlier labeled ridiculous!

Stolen Conversations

As a new parent, you may not be that different from Dan. You may wonder at making a fool of yourself. You may not understand the importance of responding to your child at her level so that she can in turn respond to you. You may carry on your conversations with your child in secret—only when others aren't around to watch you make a fool of yourself. Take comfort in the fact that you are not alone.

Parents cannot relax and coo when other adults—or even a video camera—are present! This barrier to the circle of response has made it difficult to study or even identify important ingredients of every young child's learning. In the last two decades researchers have used hidden cameras to record parent-child interaction.

Plunging into Learning

As you discover and note the stages in your child's development, you will acquire the confidence to do what probably comes naturally. And that will make you a better observer . A brief summary of some learning milestones will help to make this venture fun for you, as well as for your child.

Using this information, along with your own increasingly perceptive observations, will strengthen the circle of response with your child. In the process you will become a reflective parent, beginning first to notice "what is," and later also the "why" of both child development and parenting.

How We Learn

Young children learn through their senses. To learn they must see, hear, touch, smell, or taste. They need to poke, feel, squeeze, and drop. They need to use their bodies to make an impact on the things around them—on noises, sights, colors, objects that move, objects that can't be budged.

All babies come equipped to learn, first through seeing and hearing, then through touching and grasping, then through smelling and tasting. How much each child learns depends on the environment. It depends on the opportunities you provide that the child can absorb—new sounds, smells, sights, and tastes that differ—if only slightly—from what they have already mastered in their sensory bank, that are just a little different from knowledge already acquired. Much depends on how eagerly and confidently the child is willing to approach new opportunities.

Thinking about Thinking

The face of child development theory has changed profoundly in the past ten to fifteen years, largely through the work of the Swiss psychologist Jean Piaget. His studies on cognition (thinking and knowing) and how it develops have changed teachers' and psychologists' views of teaching and learning.

More important, Piaget's ideas have revolutionized our conception of how we learn (epistemology) and how we study the development of very young children. Although his work did not deal exclusively with early childhood, his contribution to an understanding of how very young children think has been profound. He observed infants at play and developed an intricate analysis of their problem-solving and development. His work is the basis for most present-day research in early learning, with others now building on what he began several decades ago.

The concept of dissonance mentioned earlier is basic. In a sense, all learning is generated by dissonance. We learn by challenging what we already know. That's dissonant—different. This is true for everyone—parents and children alike.

Some of what you are reading in this book contains dissonant information—different from what you already know. If you feel only a *little* dissonance, you are probably ready to read on and restructure what you know to include the new. But if you feel too much dissonance (the information is too different from what you now know), one of three things may happen:

1. You may in frustration reject the new information totally.

2. You may accept some of the new information, but only as much as "makes sense" with what you already know.

3. You may test what you read; you may re-read and/or discuss what you are reading with someone who is an "expert" (in this case, maybe a parent of a three-year-old).

Even if you accept the new information, you will probably do so only by testing the new ideas against previous experience. If you are parenting a two-year-old, much of that testing will be done against recalled experiences. In other words, what you are reading challenges you to think somewhat differently about the past two years. If you are parenting a child less than a year old or a newborn, you will compare these new ideas to your current experiences—things your baby is doing right now.

Children likewise accept or reject new ideas and experiences based on what they already know. We watch them roll over, then reach, then try to sit up, until finally they toddle under their own steam. No thinking parent encourages a child to walk who is just learning to roll over. That would be just too much dissonance, and the child would reject it. But encouraging the child to reach for your finger or a brightly colored rattle provides just the right amount of dissonance—an object not yet attainable, but within reach if the child is developing normally. You can think of many other examples of this "just right" dissonance as you care for and play with your child day by day.

Providing dissonance—and monitoring the amount—constitutes the most important support you can currently provide for your child's cognitive/conceptual development. In fact, you have the expertise. No one else treasures each new accomplishment of your new little wonder with the same interest as you do. No one else spends as much time with your baby. Infants receive their parents' attention for several hours each day, even when they are cared for outside the home for a part of each day. No one else senses all the nuances of interest and ability in the new child. You as a parent hold the title of *expert*.

Living Love

Responses to your baby or young child reinforce cognitive growth but also contribute to spiritual development. Your messages send signals of approval or disapproval—of trust or lack of trust in your child's abilities—of strength your child can depend upon. How you respond to your child's cognitive and physical accomplishments helps form the child's early concept of God. How we think of God—approving, able to be trusted, dependable—comes not only from what we read in Scripture, but also from what we have experienced. To all of us, but especially to children, hearing and reading about a loving

God makes sense largely through the example of a loving parent, or other special person, as a model for God's love.

God's love is unconditional, a fact that is hard to believe; and in a sense it is irrational (i.e., beyond reason, incomprehensible, felt but never really understood).With that kind of love your child can thrive. With an acceptance of those incomprehensible aspects of God's love, our individual relationships with God can also thrive. God's love will never make sense to natural, sinful mankind. God demonstrated His love toward us in this: "*While we were still sinners*, Christ died for us" (Rom. 5:8). Logical? Rational? Full of conditions? Prefaced by "ifs"? No! Unconditional, therefore irrational and illogical from our viewpoint.

Your own grasp of this profound and wonderful truth also came in part from your exposure to the love of God reflected by someone else—your parents, a teacher, a pastor, a friend, a spouse. How wonderful if we can offer that kind of love, that kind of dependable environment *right from the start* to our newborn infants! How wonderful that you want to learn how to give your child a solid spiritual foundation.

Starting Right

Bonding occurs very early in the relationship of the child and parents (and grandparents, if you're fortunate). This bonding or mutual attachment of affection lets the child thrive and develop in a non-threatening, supportive environment. Bonding becomes clearer when we examine what happens when it does not occur.

In the earlier part of the twentieth century, psychiatrist Rene Spitz became distressed by what he identified as infants who exhibited a "failure to thrive." He was disturbed to learn of infants in South America who had all the advantages necessary for a good start, but still failed to thrive, or even to survive. Born with normal intelligence, to the extent that it could be measured, they received adequate care. They had no major diseases. They had toys, good food, trained nursing care, and the companionship of other children. But what they lacked was significant adult interaction.

These infants lived in an orphanage, a foundling home. They received care from an overworked staff of nurses and were diapered, fed, and placed in their cribs without love and affection. Their overworked caregivers did not take time to play with them, talk to them, or stimulate their development. As a result, the foundlings actually regressed. At age two, their intelligence now was below normal, though it had been normal when they were born. They lost weight, ignored the toys provided them, and stared into space. Many of them died by age two or two-and-a-half.

Not far from this foundling home, a nursery also provided group care for infants. But these infants smiled, stayed alert, gained weight, and showed interest in the world around them. They entered the world without the advantages of the foundlings. Most were of below average intelligence, the children of uneducated mothers. Their mothers were imprisoned when these infants were born, in a facility for females adjoining the nursery. The mothers had been prostitutes, drug addicts, or thieves—not a promising legacy for a newborn! Yet these infants thrived. They grew, learned, and gained weight. Amazingly, by age two, many of them had rated a normal intelligence score.

Why did the foundlings with better parentage and higher intelligence at birth fail to develop? Why did the nursery infants without these advantages thrive? Love, adult interaction, and bonding seem to have made the difference.

The mothers cared for the nursery infants. They had an identified, primary caregiver. One special person diapered, fed, played with, and loved each child. Although prison inmates, the mothers received permission to care for their infants several hours each day. The children had other caregivers during their time in the nursery, but that special person had bonded to each of them. The mothers stimulated and spurred them on to learn. These children with several strikes against them could grow and learn.

At the foundling home, however, a staff of overworked practical nurses could do no more than feed and diaper infants all day. Cribs lined the walls. Each adult moved from child to child performing routine tasks, with very little talking or holding, busying themselves with the "essentials." These children did not learn how to hold a toy, reach for a spoon, or coo with an adult. They had no one with whom to bond. No adult was special for each child—no one to learn for and with—no love that the infant could identify.

Oh, the people cared. They kept each child clean and germ-free. They provided a sanitary environment. But they didn't know that more was needed. In the early 1900s, the high infant mortality rate at orphanages was simply accepted as an unfortunate fact of life. Until Dr. Spitz came along and questioned the status quo. He identified the missing ingredients: love and bonding to a special adult.

Love Is Your Legacy

That's what you have to offer. The relationship with your special infant began before birth. Bonding came naturally as you noticed movements, especially kicking, as you talked to your baby in the womb. For you adoptive parents, the anticipation and preparations for the child's entry into your home set the stage for a similar bonding.

Once an infant arrives and begins developing apart from Mom's body, bonding comes easiest for the natural mother. She has had nine months of close contact. But dads, adoptive parents, and even grandparents can bond, too, with just a little effort. Many fathers say that it's the first smile that does it. The infant responds and Dad bonds!

God equipped us with the ability—even the desire—to bond with our infant—and for the infant to respond. This "helpless" little creature can already see you and hear you right after birth. Researchers have discovered that two-week-old infants found the human face more interesting than other patterns and designs they were shown. Babies demonstrated this by sucking harder and more excitedly when they were shown face patterns. At two months, babies know clearly which face goes with which voice and can become upset if they see a face but hear a voice that doesn't belong with it.

Very early—probably at or before birth—the infant hears voices and begins to distinguish Mother's voice. Two factors may account for this. Baby lived close to Mother's voice for nine months and heard it regularly while still in the womb. So that voice sounds familiar at birth. Interestingly, the baby seems to have the ability to hear high vocal registers first—a soprano rather than a bass voice. This means that Mother's voice is more clearly audible to a newborn. God's provision includes both the baby's ability to hear and Mom's ability to breastfeed and, therefore, to spend more time with the new child.

This means that Dad should learn to elevate the pitch of his voice when he talks to his new baby—something people often do without knowing why. My voice has an alto register. I've been pitching my voice higher to talk to babies for years. Only recently did I learn that the baby needs this to be able to hear me well. It was a thrill to discover that something I do naturally is actually important for the child developmentally. Another evidence of God's wonderful provision!

Building a Legacy

The first three years are extremely important for child development. How you respond to your child's mastery of new tasks, how you encourage new learning, can determine how your child approaches new tasks and learning for a lifetime. Therefore provide manageable challenges, interesting new tasks. Provide toys and activities that keep frustration under control. Let your child struggle—within reason—with a new skill before offering clues that will lead to mastery. Applaud each new accomplishment with enthusiasm and approval. Praise attempts that fail, too. Every young child needs to know that effort is important—and doesn't automatically lead to success.

All of these techniques enhance social, emotional, physical, and cognitive growth. Reinforcing these areas of development simultaneously lays a foundation for spiritual growth. It supports the young child's faith, growing from baptism, nurtured by God's Word.

So you're not an expert! Learn all you can about the development of young children. Read books and magazine articles. For understanding and inspiration become involved in a support group such as the *Right from the Start* Parenting Program (see inside back cover for details). Remember that spiritual development thrives in a relationship where loving parents applaud and encourage new learning. "Train up a child in the way he should go, and when he is old he will not depart from it" (Prov. 22:6). Your task as a new parent is to understand what a child can do and to know how to challenge and encourage along the way. Help your child learn about God and His love for us. Help your child learn to love God—**right from the start!**

CHAPTER THREE

Specially Created for You

Who Is This Child?

Your child is *special,* created by God. Almost from the moment of birth, you have been able to see family traits in this new little person. She may have Mom's eyes, Dad's smile, Grandma's nose, Grandpa's forehead. Or the characteristics came in a slightly different mix. Or maybe what you have begun to see in this infant is Dad's ability to relax, Mom's curiosity and zest, or the giggle and wit of one of the grandparents.

In any case, what you are seeing is the *person* that was born to you, not just the baby. How exciting to know that this little one is already a person!

When Diane was a newborn, I spent a week in the hospital, in traction for back spasms and pain. Diane was already at home, being cared for by a woman named Diana. My long-distance parenting was certainly stressful, but the week was soon over and we were back together. But it was several weeks before Diane and I (and Bob, of course) were on our own. Meanwhile it was good to have Diana around to perform many of the routine tasks I was not yet allowed to do. I listened to her conversations with little Diane. One day, as she brought Diane to me, she said, "Here's your little 'people,' ready for some hugs from Mom." And to Diane she said, "Soon you'll be a person, but now you're just a 'people.' We don't really know who you'll be yet."

"Wait a minute," I thought. "She's a person right now! I've already had nine months to get used to her activity level and to sense her responses to noise!" But since Diana was the experienced parent with two children and I the novice, I said nothing.

But that little interchange with Diane and Diana I've

never forgotten. After studying infancy and child development, I *know* that I was right. Diane wasn't *becoming* a person. She already *was* a person—an individual with likes and dislikes (it didn't take long for anyone to know that she didn't like her feet to be bound in any way!), a person who loved to talk to herself, especially to her tiny fingers, a person who wanted to be perched somewhere where she could watch the going and coming around her.

Your child, too, is a person. An individual not only with unique fingerprints and footprints, but an individual with unique activity patterns and unique responses to touch, sight, and sound. Your child is a unique person with an already unique *person*ality in place, waiting to be discovered and observed by you. That *person*ality includes your baby's approach to both new and familiar experiences, a level of contentment when left alone to play, curiosity, zest, and smiles.

Baby Styles

Each new child is created by God. No two are alike. We all know that. But I'm not sure we understand how unique and complex each of these creations really is.

Each baby comes into the world—even into the womb—as a unique creation of God. The *person* that will later be a child and an adult is already there! As a baby, each has a style, a way of behaving and reacting, that is uniquely and specially his or her own. The style may be active or passive. It may include a high or low sensitivity to noise, a keen awareness of the surrounding sights, or a greater awareness to smells and touch.

Dr. Berry Brazelton, a famous pediatrician, has asserted in several writings that a baby's personality traits can be identified as early as two weeks after birth. He studied the child's zest and the responsiveness to smiles, challenges, and new experiences. He looked at the child's activity level, the desire for new experiences, and the level of contentment. In each of these areas he identified traits which later emerged as a part of that baby's personality.

As I watch young infants and think back to my own, I know he is right. In fact, I think that some traits, such as activity level, can be identified before birth.

Infant specialists also believe that ways of approaching the world are already in place from the beginning. Some babies are strong-willed, some rather compliant and agreeable. Others can be described as sunny and full of zest.

Ways of Thinking

Very early in life, all of us have our own special ways of thinking about events around us. Some of us are keenly aware of details about us and remember particular aspects of past events for a long time. Others are less likely to remember details but have soaked up the overall, or global, event. We may not grasp all the details (I'm one of these!), but we're good at the big picture and the message or meaning of events.

When it comes to doing, some of us need to have all details firmly in place before we feel comfortable, while others are quite content if the big picture is right, and we don't get bogged down in every detail. Details often get in the way for the global people; and detailists don't bother about overall perspective. Each needs the other.

Ways of Taking In

In addition to our unique ways of thinking, each of us has different ways of taking in the world and the events in it. Some are sight-oriented, some sound-oriented, some movement- and touch-oriented. The sight-oriented are visual learners; the sound-oriented are auditory learners; and the touch- and movement-oriented are called kinesthetic learners.

Sight people, who tend to focus on what they see, even use words like "focus" and "see" more frequently than others as they talk and write! They are strongly aware of color, pattern, and design—anything their eyes can take in.

Sound people tend to hear sounds before they focus on the visible and are often very noise-sensitive. They are happiest working with the radio or stereo in the background.

Touch people become actively involved in doing, focusing on actions, feelings, tastes, or smells of an experience or event.

Your baby has already begun to address the world as a sight-, sound-, or touch-person and already responds more actively and positively to one of these stimuli than to the other two. To make the matter even more complex, she has a second way of taking things in. As you watch your baby, you'll notice that she first uses her eyes to see, then her ears to hear a new toy or event. Or she may be more interested in what the toy does or how it moves before she notices the noise it makes. Or she may focus first on sound and then on either sight or touch.

As you observe her learning pattern, you'll even find yourself calling attention to the things she's likely to notice first! Your sensitivity as parents to the "taking-in" or learning styles is an important ability that God has given you to help your baby learn.

Ways of Doing

In addition to ways of taking in and ways of thinking, your baby also has a unique way of approaching her exploration and learning. She may plunge into every new experience with confidence and zest, willing to try anything, interested in what makes things go, testing out a variety of possibilities for every new situation. That kind of child is an experimenter.

She may be more ready to approach the world with a wait-and-see attitude, happy to observe before doing, often needing to be sure she can do it right before even trying. It's almost as if she tests the task internally before she does it. This child is an internalizer.

Or she may be a child who uses her mouth constantly—to suck, to coo, to babble, to accompany everything she does. It's almost as if she needs to put her tongue in gear before the rest of her can do anything. (When she's three or four, this is the child that will most likely "cut with her tongue" while she cuts with the scissors!) As this infant starts to crawl and walk, you'll always know where she is, because she's probably making noise with her mouth as she goes along. This child is most definitely a verbalizer, and it almost seems as if the mouth is a necessary tool for thinking!

Your Child, A Special Child

Think about you own little child for a moment. Which ways of thinking, taking-in, and doing are you beginning to notice? Have you found yourself emphasizing those unique styles without even knowing it? That's tuning in to your baby! That's *synchrony.*

Bonding is the tie or cord of affection and love between parent and child. Synchrony, however, is that but goes beyond to include an intuitive and informed response to your child's unique baby style or *person*ality!

Your child is a person, created by God in His image—special to you, special to God. Your child already has a personality which is becoming more and more evident to you as you watch your child grow.

Our youngest child, Lynelle, is definitely a sight-person. As a very young infant she was happy to be propped up so that she could watch the going and coming of those around her. At that time I probably took that style for granted (and thanked God for an agreeable third child!), but today I can see/identify her penchant for watching as a clue to her visual and internalizing style of learning.

Her approach to events today could have been identified two decades ago if I had known about baby styles when she was a baby! But though I didn't know all this at that time, I did many of the "right" things as I responded to her *person*ality. God provided the ability to bond and to respond in synchrony, even though I did not have the labels for what was happening. How much more exciting for you, now that you have the labels for what you are doing as you support your child's early journey in *person*hood.

God's View

It may be useful to look for a moment at what Jesus had to say about children in order to help us appreciate the importance of the children He entrusts to us. In His ministry, Jesus welcomed children to His side. He even scolded His disciples for attempting to prevent the children from "bothering" Jesus. He went on to say, "The kingdom of God belongs to such as these" (Matt. 19:14).

This statement becomes even more powerful when we know that in the years before Christ both the Greek and Roman cultures did not consider children to be fully human until about age seven. Therefore, if a child did not survive infancy and early childhood, the loss was easier to tolerate. Since infant mortality was high, this cultural attitude may have served as a protective support for parents.

Another story about Jesus and children adds more insight. When the disciples needed to be corrected because they argued about who would be the greatest in heaven, Jesus put a little child in the middle of the group and told them they needed to become like this child (whom others still considered sub-human) in order to enter heaven. That couldn't have been easy for them to accept.

The Most Special Child

Knowing what people in Jesus' day thought of children, let's look at the Bible's account of Jesus' childhood. Although the Bible says little about His infancy and childhood, we have enough that can be instructive for us.

We all know the story of Jesus' birth in a stable—a

humble beginning. But note that the shepherds, when told of Jesus' birth by angels, left their flocks to hurry and see this Special Child! A most unusual thing for a group of shepherds to do under any circumstances, but absolutely mind-boggling if we remember that people then usually regarded babies as less than fully human!

Note what Luke then reports. In the custom of that time, Jesus was taken to the temple on the eighth day of His life. Every firstborn male child (who "opened the womb" of his mother) was to be called holy. So Mary and Joseph went to Jerusalem, not too far from Bethlehem, to the temple.

What happened next, however, was significant. In the temple two people, Simeon and Anna—both of them very old—were waiting for God's promise of the Savior to be fulfilled. When Mary and Joseph brought Jesus into the temple, Simeon took the Baby in his arms and said, "Lord, my eyes have seen Your salvation." (Remember the prevailing attitude toward infants.) By the power of the Holy Spirit Simeon knew that this little Child was the Savior Jesus, who would take away his sin—and the sin of all people. Even more, he knew that this Infant was God.

Luke says that Anna, too, gave thanks for this Infant and told everyone whom she knew that their wait for the Messiah was over! Though Simeon and Anna saw only the infant Jesus, not the mature adult, by God's Holy Spirit they could say that Jesus was the Messiah, God become man.

The references to children in the Bible may be limited, especially in the New Testament, but each is powerful and instructive. All children are special. Jesus Himself said we should take on childlike traits. In our walk with God our children can teach us in matters of faith, trust, and love. Study your child. Learn from your child. Walk the way of faith with your child. Take your specially created child by the hand and walk with Jesus *right from the start.*

CHAPTER FOUR

In God's Image

You—Your Self

God has made each of us unique—special! There isn't another person quite like you. There certainly isn't another person quite like your baby!

Maybe you're short, maybe tall. Maybe you're thin, maybe overweight. Maybe your skin is deep rosy brown, or golden olive, or pale yellow or creamy white. Your outward features are a part of who *you* are.

But a much greater part, a more influential part of what makes *you* is that elusive thing called *self*. Who *you* are depends much on who you have become, and how you feel about your *self*. Psychologists and educators refer to the "feeling about self" as your self-concept.

If your self-concept is positive, you are generally happy with yourself. You consider yourself a capable, competent human being. You know that you sin, but you forgive yourself because you know that Jesus forgives you. You are willing to try again and fully expect that "next time" will be better. And if it isn't, you're willing to forgive yourself again and try once more.

If you have a poor self-concept, you are unhappy. You may wish that you were taller, thinner, shorter, or fatter. You're not so sure that you're very competent at anything. You approach each new event or project with fear. You can't forgive yourself for any wrong you have done. Sometimes it's even hard to accept God's forgiveness.

Self-Concept

Much of your self-concept was formed as a child. What your parents and other "important" people said to you and about you helped you think of your self as an "I can" or an "I can't" person. Your self is at least in part a mirror of how your parents and other adults regarded you and your abilities during your childhood.

Now it's your turn. Obviously, you want to nurture a positive self-concept in your child. The challenge comes in knowing how to do it.

First, consider that the self is formed bit by bit through the experiences and challenges that are encountered. The success—or, more correctly, the *feeling* of success—in those experiences is critical. The feeling comes from the reactions of the significant people in the child's world—parents, grandparents, or daytime caregivers.

If early attempts at walking, one tottering step after another, are cheered and applauded, the child gains a desire to try again. Conversely, when the first steps go almost unnoticed, the child has little motivation to repeat the attempt. It's no fun to totter and fall without an appreciative audience!

The child who is cheered on for simply trying, though success is barely evident, gains confidence and feels good about trying because just trying pleases the adults.

I Think I Can

Very early the child absorbs and mirrors adults' attitudes of approval or disapproval. Your responses to her earliest smiles and cooings send messages of pleasure and approval—or lack of it. Your return smiles and cooings tell your baby that she is important. Getting a response from you—a smile, "ga-ga," or "pretty baby"—tells her, "I can," even before she holds up her head without support!

This positive view of self is built piece by piece through the little things you do each day. It grows with verbal play and cooing, and when you encourage physical feats of sitting up, rolling over, and walking. It opens up when you encourage problem-solving—how to get a rattle that's out of reach, how to put nesting blocks inside each other, or how to assemble a simple puzzle.

As the child grows, problem-solving tasks become more complex and more time-consuming. If you wish to promote an "I can" attitude, you must supply time and patience for her to do things by herself. Learning independence is also important for a healthy self-concept. Your baby's first attempts at feeding herself are hard to tolerate. It's much neater and faster to do it yourself. Who wants to clean up spinach or green beans from the hair, the table, and the floor—even if they are strained vegetables? But self-feeding, though slow and messy, brings a sense of accomplishment—"I can!" She won't get it any other way.

The same holds true for learning to dress herself. You can encourage your two-year-old to help pull up her slacks or to pull on her socks after you have positioned them on her toes. She can choose whether to wear the blue or the red shirt. It takes longer than doing it yourself. But it sends a message of support as she absorbs your confidence in her budding abilities. You are building an "I can" person and nourishing a positive self-concept.

Freedom to Fail

The path of accomplishments is not always smooth. Your child will attempt many things without immediate success. In fact, she may encounter failure repeatedly before having success. How your child responds to failure depends very much on you.

You will be the child's model for coping with frustration and failure. If you become impatient with her frustration, so will your child. If you become angry with her failure, so will your child.

If, on the other hand, your actions and attitudes show that failure is an avenue to learning and that frustration can be managed, you are on the right track. You are teaching that not every attempt will be met with success, that trying is as important as succeeding.

The noted author Madelaine L'Engle has written how

the attitudes she acquired in early childhood affected her response to life. *A Wrinkle in Time*, written for children, was rejected by publishers for two years before one finally accepted it. The fourteen rejection letters were symbols of failure. Her response was to try again, partly because of attitudes that she had learned from her parents.

A Wrinkle in Time was finally published and won the annual Newbery medal of the American Library Association for the best children's book of the year—after the author's struggling two years for acceptance.

What if Madelaine L'Engle had given up with the first, or even the fifth, rejection? It must have been tempting. That amount of rejection cannot be easy for anyone to tolerate, even for a published author. I'm sure that most of us would have given up much sooner.

All of us seek acceptance and risk rejection each day, though it may be less dramatic than Madelaine L'Engle's experience. Each time you submit a completed project to a supervisor or co-worker, you hope for acceptance and risk rejection. When suggesting a new idea to a colleague or friend, you seek acceptance and risk rejection.

Some seldom venture a suggestion because the risk is too great. The possibility of rejection and failure looms too large.

Encouraging Risks

I often watch infants and parents in grocery stores, shopping malls, and especially airports. People sometimes wait for hours at airports. That wait with young children can be instructional. How they deal with the child's boredom and frustration often says much about how and what that child is learning about success and failure.

Some time ago I watched a two-year-old attempt to open the latch on the travel bag at her mother's feet. She knew the bag contained snacks and she wanted some. She twisted the knot several times without success. Her mother watched smiling. Several times the child looked to her mother for help. Each time Mom smiled and nodded, "You can do it, Kimmie." With a look of increased determination, Kimmie would try once more.

After several more tries, Kimmie almost opened the latch. Almost, but not quite. "Oh," said Kimmie's mom. "You almost had it that time. Good girl!" She then opened the latch for Kimmie, took out a piece of dried fruit for her to chew, and closed the travel bag. Kimmie happily chewed her piece of fruit and enjoyed the reward for her hard work.

Within a few minutes she was hard at work again, trying to open the latch. The challenge of the task was becoming more important than the reward.

Kimmie kept up this activity for almost half an hour. Each time she appeared to be overcome by frustration, her mother would comment or smile approval. Encouragement seemed to be all that Kimmie needed. She continued to work, satisfied with an occasional reward of a snack or a treasure from the contents of the bag. Kimmie was learning to cope with frustration. She was learning to meet failure without failing.

Weeks later I was waiting at the same airport. Again I watched the interaction of a parent and child. While 18-month-old Sammy and his mother waited for a plane, Sammy pulled a duck on wheels behind himself as he toddled around the waiting area. Whenever he changed directions, the duck fell on its side and no longer quacked as it rolled along behind Sammy. Each time the duck fell, his mother walked over to Sammy and righted the duck for him. "Poor Sammy," she would say, "you can't make the duck stay up."

After several repetitions of this sequence and the negative message, "You can't do it yourself," Sammy's mother tired of the task. She refused to walk over to Sammy and fix the duck. "No," she said, "I'm too tired. I can't now." Sammy sadly looked at the fallen duck, then dragged it along. He tried once or twice to right the duck himself, but the task seemed insurmountable. "Can't," he said, and dragged it over to his mother. Sammy's mother righted the duck once again and went back to the magazine she was reading.

Sammy and Kimmie received different messages in these waiting room scenarios. One of them absorbed the beginnings of an "I can't yet, but I'll try" attitude toward difficult tasks. The other learned that he needed help for difficult tasks and wouldn't be able to master them alone—even worse, that trying could become an insurmountable obstacle.

Both Sammy and Kimmie were learning for life—one positively, the other negatively. The attitude and encouragement of Kimmie's mom could launch her toward a life of trying and eventually succeeding. Sammy's mom, however, taught him that life was difficult and frustrating, not always worth the effort. He was learning to wait for things to happen for him.

A World View

These opposing views of life are likely to become each child's self-image, especially if similar experiences are repeated regularly and frequently. Such early experiences become a part of each child's definition of self.

Though each of us since the fall is inclined to sin, we were all created in the image of God for His glory (Is. 43:7). He has loved each of us with an everlasting love (Jer. 31:3). If *God* can love us, we certainly ought to be able to love our*selves*, to regard our *selves* as worth loving. He loved us while we were yet sinners (1 John 4:10), in spite of our sin. He sent His only Son Jesus to pay for that sin. As a result, we can love Him "because He first loved us" (1 John 4:19).

This special person—your child—has been created and is loved by God. Now she is to be loved by you. She can be helped to regard herself as worthy of that love and to appreciate herself as a lovable creation of God. What a legacy we have from God! What a legacy we can pass on to our children! Right from the start!

THE FAITH

CHAPTER FIVE

Touching the Heart

Your child's view of life is formed during the early years and lasts a lifetime. It can be shaped by attitudes of hope, optimism, and joy—or negativism, pessimism, and despair. Which shall it be?

There's no question what you want for your child. Of course you opt for hope, optimism, and joy. But which are you providing—negativism or hope?—pessimism or optimism?—despair or joy?

Are you concentrating on happy experiences and surrounding your child with faith-building activities? Is your child absorbing an attitude toward life that centers on optimism? How optimistic and hopeful is your own view?

Do you "rejoice in hope" (Rom. 12:12)? Is hope the "anchor of your soul" (Heb. 6:19)? Our hope is in God and comes from God (Ps. 39:7; 2 Thess. 2:16). It fills us with joy and peace (Rom. 15:13). It gives us confidence and a solid basis for rejoicing (Heb. 3:6). Hope in God prompts and persuades us to be happy and nurtures an attitude of optimism. The Holy Spirit directs and guides us into the future, the otherwise dreaded unknown, with confidence and trust.

Yet it is not enough that you yourself live in optimism and hope. Your child must also see it, feel it, sense it, and experience it.

Personalizing God's Love

I was taken to church regularly as an infant. I was expected as a toddler to participate in—"sit through"—the adult worship service Sunday after Sunday. For many, that can become intolerable if the experience becomes a power struggle between Mom's expectations and the toddler's squirmings.

But I was fortunate. I remember those Sunday services with warmth and a smile. They were happy experiences imprinted in my storehouse of memories.

I'm sure I was a normal, wiggly toddler. My mother did not allow me to roam the pews during the sermon (which I have witnessed, sad to say!). But this former wiggly toddler does have happy memories of those early years in church.

I was fortunate to have a personal and personalized interest in the prayers, hymns, liturgy, and even the sermon each week. Let me explain.

During all my growing-up years, our church was blessed to have a well-loved and articulate pastor—a humble but eloquent preacher. His well-constructed sermons were Biblical, logically outlined, and elegantly constructed with rich, formal English. They were also eloquently delivered.

Every Sunday Pastor Bickel delivered a sermon with flawless grammar. He used language that echoed the phrases of the King James Bible. Each Sunday he made a point of repeating words and phrases from Bible passages that school children were memorizing. And they eagerly listened for those passages. Formal language, but elegant, eloquent, and meaningful.

His messages were meaningful for me even as a toddler. You see, one of Pastor Bickel's favorite words—formal, but elegant—was "surely." "*Surely* we can know this because He sent His Son, Jesus," he would say. "*Surely* we have a certain hope of salvation," he would continue. He never used "certainly"—always "surely." This constituted a small but significant detail for a toddler whose name was Shirley—a toddler who was convinced that the pastor was saying her name—was talking right to her— each Sunday. Her pastor talked to her not just sometimes—but each Sunday—several times each Sunday!

I remember standing on the pew beside my mother, or sitting on her lap, and raising my hand to make sure the pastor could see me. Sometimes to make absolutely certain of his attention—and maybe his awareness of my attention—I would shout out my name in response to hearing it as he preached.

I must have been a trial to my parents as I listened actively—and responded eagerly—to the sermon each week. But the happy memories of sermons—messages from God—specially delivered right to me each Sunday have left a lifetime impression. Sermons are still special messages to me, which I listen to and anticipate with gladness. Worship is a joyful and personal experience, no matter how formal the service.

Today I still worship occasionally in the church where I heard those "special" sermons decades ago. The pastor who delivered them is with his Savior. But each time I return "home" to that church, a sense of happiness and acceptance washes over me. That sanctuary, those pews hold special warmth—almost love—for the toddler become adult who experienced a special and unique personalization of God's love there.

Building Experiences

Not all young children can have that special experience. (But be aware of it for a Grace, a Joy, a Daniel, or Paul, or David!) Yet each child can happily—and even noisily—participate in the "amens," the songs (there's nothing wrong with singing "la-la-la" before they know the words), the greeting of peace. Allow your child to store up happy memories of worship—to begin to love God's house before he can even say the word—to participate actively in the worship activities of the faith community into which he has been born!

Imprinting happy memories begins in the earliest pre-toddler days with the experiences you offer your baby that capture and express your joy in Jesus—your worship as well as your prayer—your living as well as your loving— your smiles as well as your words.

The music that your child hears as an infant is a good place to start. Learn some lullabies. Search your memory for those songs of comfort that were sung to you in your earliest days. Sing hymns that have a happy, comforting melody. Your newborn won't understand the words you're singing, but she will absorb the feelings of trust and hope which the words and melody convey.

As soon as your child is ready to participate in ritual, be sure to include her in prayer. At first her participation will be limited to the actions—folded hands and quiet listening. But the sense of being included in something important and special will transcend those simple actions. Your child will absorb your attitudes of hope and trust by being included in your conversations with the Lord.

Share with your child your own reactions of praise and thanks for the little gifts God gives us each day— your joy in a beautiful sunset, your delight in a new flower just starting to bud, your pleasure in the warmth of a sunny day, your thanks for the rain to nourish the earth. Include an audible "Thank You, Lord" or an "Isn't God good to us?" to help your child sense the source of your hope and joy.

Give your child a sensory legacy of positive attitudes. As adults we often react irrationally to certain sights, sounds, smells, touches, even tastes. As children we were probably exposed to these same sensory experiences in either very positive or very negative circumstances.

There is little logic in an adult's reaction to certain floral scents. Adult reactions in many instances can be traced to early sensory memories and the attitudes and events that surrounded them.

I have a friend who becomes momentarily depressed when he smells carnations or chrysanthemums. He associates them with funerals and death. His grandparents both died when he was quite young—age two and age five. According to the practice in some parts of the country fifty or more years ago, the caskets—and the flowers— were placed in the home of the deceased, or of an offspring of the deceased with a large enough home. In the case of my friend, his parents had the largest living room, or parlor, as it was then called. So their home was used for the wake, the place for friends and relatives to come to offer sympathy and "pay their respects."

Many bouquets of flowers would be placed in this parlor—especially carnations and chrysanthemums. So my friend still associates the scent of those flowers with death and sadness. His reaction becomes understandable when you know the source.

Another person might react quite positively to the same flowers, or to other varieties. My husband has filled our yard with many, many flowers, creating borders all around the house and between our yard and those of both neighbors with his favorite flowers, daisies and deep bronze gaillardias. The sight (neither has a strong scent) of these flowers gives him a feeling of security and peace.

Why? His grandmother's back yard was filled with these flowers, also in a neat border. Their sight evokes a memory of the security and love she showed him during his childhood. His early experiences with flowers go with us whenever we enter a church or select flowers for the church altar to commemorate or celebrate a family event.

Candles are another example of objects that evoke "illogical" reactions in the lives of some. I react differently to them than Bob. In my childhood, candles were always used on birthday cakes—long tapers—and were lit for special meals and for company. In Bob's childhood, candles seem to have been considered a frill. His family had only a single, elegant pair on the dining room table—and unlit. He has learned not to comment when I light candles or decorate a birthday cake each year, but I know he considers them unnecessary and extravagant. For me, they are a symbol of graciousness, hospitality, and fun. For other families, candles become symbols of family prayer and sharing.

For many, the sound of organ music is associated with worship and praise. After a long time I have accepted the idea that home organs can be used for "secular" as well as sacred music. Others have needed even more time to recognize the guitar as an appropriate instrument for sacred music! Our earliest experiences later evoke an almost subconscious reaction and attitude for many, many years. That may in part explain vehement reactions to Christian rock music!

Imprinting Happy Memories

By now you should be convinced that you can have a positive influence on your baby's attitudes and reactions, both to the commonplace and to the profound. As you build routines and rituals that are pleasing and pleasurable, you are imprinting a positive outlook on life in your child's storehouse of memories. These memories will affect your child's openness to new experiences for a lifetime.

It isn't possible—or even desirable—to provide a smorgasbord of experiences for your child that is always pleasant and new experiences that are always openly received. We want our children to be exposed to life as it is, to be discriminating, and to learn to avoid potential danger and harm. But it is possible to provide a majority of pleasurable experiences that will on balance produce the hope and optimism you are trying to weave into the fabric of your child's personality.

Certain activities and sensory experiences will be more important than others for your growing family. You will probably choose some activities rationally and have clearly articulated reasons for doing so. Other activities will have an emotional loading creeping in from your own childhood and will seem illogical to everyone but you.

I have a colleague whose roots are deeply embedded in the culture of Lithuania where her parents were born. She became fluent in both English and Lithuanian. But today when she sees an infant, she has an overwhelming urge to coo and babble to the baby in Lithuanian. She now has two young children of her own. Both are learning Lithuanian as well as English. Both heard their first lullabies in Lithuanian—from their mother as well as from their grandmother. She says it just doesn't feel right to comfort a baby in English.

This same colleague discovered her identification of Lithuanian with the young when she was a preschool teacher. She soon realized that she had to translate favorite nursery rhymes and songs into English before she could use them in her classroom!

Such an association, binding a certain language with young children, attests to the power of early sensory experiences. My friend's recollections of sound and touch (as she was being rocked and soothed) are so powerful that in situations where English is the more appropriate language, she must concentrate in order to suppress her intuitive use of the language that is tied to her happy early memories.

For another person, Lithuanian or another secondary language could arouse memories of unhappiness or confusion. The key is the emotional aura surrounding the language.

Happy experiences produce happy memories, a storehouse of satisfied, joyful emotions that generate positive attitudes toward new experiences. As your child stores up these happy memories, he is accumulating evidence that the world is a good place to be, that good things are likely to continue to happen.

Making a Memory Bank

How you go about building up those happy memories for your child depends on you. You will make some choices based on your own early experiences. Others you will make because you know they will have a positive impact on your child.

However you choose to build up those happy memories, remember that they become a part of the fabric of your child's attitudes and will by and large be special memories. They tend to come from frequently repeated events and activities that you by your love have reinforced.

As your child learns trust in the world through pre-

44

dictable events, he learns to trust in a God who is predictable and loving. As your child learns to hope for good experiences through contact with dependable adults, he learns to hope in the Lord, and to find joy in that hope.

Faith is reciprocally built on hope, and implicit in hope. Faith and hope are *essentially* interrelated. Your child's faith development is nurtured through experiences that build an attitude of hope. How you build hope depends upon you—your own childhood experiences, your own priorities, and what you choose to provide for your child. You have already started to weave your child's attitudes, sometimes consciously, sometimes unconsciously.Chapter eleven has specific suggestions for activities and rituals that will help build faith, *right from the start.*

CHAPTER SIX

Seeing the Unseen

For most new parents, an infant's faith or spiritual development is a rather nebulous, abstract idea. You have made sure that your child has been baptized into the faith of the Triune God. Your child has been brought to God's altar to be named and made God's own, and is now a forgiven and cleansed child of God.

But what happens next? Is this child's spiritual growth to be left to chance for the next three years?

"Wait a minute," you say. "I'm not leaving it to chance. I'm leaving it to God. There's not much I can teach this baby about faith for the next three years, so I'll put the whole problem in God's hands. Let Him worry about it! It's more than I can even comprehend."

There's the problem. The concept of faith is so difficult to grasp that we just give up. We hide behind the cliche, "It's in God's hands." Or we pretend the problem doesn't exist.

What *is* faith? Can you see it? If not, how can you understand something you can't even see? That is a real problem—seeing the unseen. How do you apply what God says in His Word to the day-to-day life of diapering and burping, cooing and cuddling?

The Evidence

But we *can* know faith! We know from our own experience. We know faith by what God has told us about it in His Word. We know it by its evidence.

When my first child began to move inside me enough so that I could feel her movements, I couldn't see her with my eyes. I couldn't see those arms reaching out as they poked the sides of my uterus. I couldn't see those legs give the kick that protruded from my stomach, sometimes at an embarrassing moment. I couldn't see what was causing the ripples of discomfort, those aching ribs, those black and blue marks.

But I knew those arms and legs were there. I knew that body was moving around. I knew it was getting bigger because the kicks were getting bigger. I knew by the *evidence*!

I could imagine in my mind's eye the little arm with its fist clenched, reaching out to get more space. In my imagination I could see the tiny fingers stretching out as the body inside me turned around to find a more comfortable position. I could visualize the small knee straightening out to get a little exercise—one, two, three, four—she had started counting long before she knew the meaning of counting! I could see and feel the little foot pushing out with all its might to stretch the space available. I could imagine her whole body rolling over to try a new spot, then settling in again in comfort.

What I couldn't imagine was whether I was feeling Diane or Dion—a girl or a boy—that was stretching my body to its limits. How big would this baby be? Some questions were unanswerable. But her presence was there—unmistakably. She was growing. She was moving. She was stretching—with gusto! There was no doubt that the child I was carrying was full of energy. There has never been any doubt since she was born that she is a bundle of energy demanding to be unleashed!

I knew Diane, though yet unseen. She was hoped for and loved. She was anticipated with joy. And growing. I could tell. She was developing. I just knew it. My own powers or intervention had nothing to do with it. I was just the instrument. I couldn't change the course or the progress of development. I couldn't add a fingernail or an eyelash. I could feed her with a healthy diet, nourish her with adequate rest, encourage her with happy thoughts. But my biggest task was an acceptance of her growth, a willingness to be used by God. Unseen, I could feed her, nourish her, encourage her. But I couldn't see her. She was visible only by the *evidence*, though visible sometimes by the pain.

Seeing through Faith

So it is with faith—visible by the evidence—seeable sometimes by the pain. Your child's faith comes from and grows by God's power, not by your own. But your child's faith is fed, nourished, and encouraged by what *you* do or don't do.

Faith is the substance of those things which we hope for (Heb. 11:1). It comes by the power of God (1 Cor. 2:5), by hearing God's Word (Rom. 10:17), and is central to the way we live (Gal. 2:20).

Faith is seen not by the action of a kick or a poke (as an unborn baby is "seen"), but by the presence of its companions: hope, love, joy, and peace.

Again, our task is to be the instrument. We are called to feed, nourish, and encourage. We are to love and model God's love. We will labor together with God (1 Cor. 3:9) as we feed, nourish, and encourage.

Guiding the faith journey of your child is the single most important task ahead of you in the coming months and years. You were chosen by God to nurture this child. Your home, your Christian home, was chosen by Him as an environment for your child's development.

"Now what?" you ask. "How do I provide that environment?" Once again, God hasn't left us without a clue.

"Bring the young children to Jesus," He tells us through the gospel writers. Jesus told mothers to bring the crawlers, too. It's challenging, almost bewildering, as you contemplate how to bring crawlers to Jesus.

We know faith comes by hearing, and hearing comes through the Word of God (Rom. 10:17). Even very young children need to *hear* about God. They need to hear about His love and must hear about His care. They *can* hear mealtime prayers, bedtime prayers, and spontaneous prayers before they can form the words themselves. So they should *hear* hymns, psalms, and spiritual songs, as well as stories. For this they need to be surrounded by the evidence of the faith of their parents.

Each child needs to know God through his parents' relationship with a real, loving God. She can glimpse and grasp the trust that comes from a daily walk with God by observing the day-to-day experience of a mother and a father who have chosen the path with God.

Just as *we* know faith by its evidence, so a child, too, knows faith by the evidence in the home. Does he see your faith? Feel it? Does he grasp the evidence? Does he experience faith through you? Can he see your faith through what happens in your home day by day?

Each child's everyday experiences build a storehouse, a reservoir that can be tapped for future understanding. Your provision for a faithful relationship with your child forms a critical foundation for your child's spiritual understanding, both now and later. Your walk of faith and trust is essential to your child's spiritual growth. Providing a trusting and trustworthy environment for your child becomes an avenue leading to a developing faith in God.

The Experience of Trust

The American psychologist Erik Erikson has theorized that during the first two years of life the child's major need is to develop trust. The child learns whom to trust and how to trust. The child needs to build a preponderance of trust experiences as opposed to mistrust. This comes by experiencing and learning from the trustworthy care of a loving adult. Although Erikson is not interested in the implications for Christianity, his findings can help us understand how Christian faith develops.

Trust develops early in a young child. It begins at birth, starting with a trustworthy, dependable relationship with the mother—if the child is fed when hungry and then gets enough food. It involves being able to suck the mother's breast (or bottle) as long and as often as needed, to suckle and be cuddled.

For Christians, *trust* is more than the general reliance and hope that Erikson talks about. It is a very specific trust in God because of Jesus Christ and empowered by the work of the Holy Spirit.

Being Trustworthy

The early relationship of trust continues with the child's experience, for example, of being kept warm and dry. That includes being diapered regularly, being kept warm enough or cool enough—generally comfortable. It requires having someone dependably respond to a cry that says, "I'm wet and I really don't like it!" It means having that diaper rash tended to promptly.

An establishment of trust grows with the holding and cuddling that both Mom and Dad almost instinctively do on the first day. It develops when being held close enough to hear a heartbeat—a sound that has been so familiar for the past nine months. It unfolds with being held firmly and lovingly, and feeling firm support by the way he is being held. It requires being held often, without regard to warnings of "spoiling"!

The internalization of an attitude of trust develops as the child experiences and senses the ways in which her parents—*you*—respond to her frustrations. But what happens when life doesn't go her way, when she has to struggle just a little, when the toy she wants is just slightly out of reach? Do you rush to fix everything? Or does your child learn little by little that sometimes struggle and frustration are a part of life? Your child can learn that struggle makes attainment of the goal all the more satisfying and that frustration can be managed. Your child can trust that her parents are there to monitor the level of frustration and the amount of struggle—to keep things manageable and within bounds.

As your child learns to walk, you don't always rush to help as he confronts an obstacle or has to figure out how to walk around the corner of the table. You allow a little struggle and frustration. That is how learning takes place. But you do monitor the amount of struggle and frustration. You keep them manageable.

That is an example of being trustworthy, of monitoring the environment to keep the stress manageable. In a sense, you are modeling God's relationship with each of us. He doesn't allow any of us to be tested beyond what we are able "to bear" or manage. With our frustrations and struggles, He also gives us the "way of escape"—the resources and the ability to deal with the problem (1 Cor. 10:13). So what you are modeling for your young child is very important. The experience you provide day by day as you help your child to establish trust in you, in her surroundings, and in God is decisive for the future.

Into the Unknown

Your child's beginning trust is an important step toward living in hope. Only with trust in a dependable environment can your baby feel secure enough to hope.

Hope is an attitude about the future, about the unknown, as we work and plan each day for a tomorrow that is not completely revealed to us. God gives us one day at a time. We reach for the unknown because we are able to hope.

When your child begins to greet the world with hope, as opposed to fear, you have the evidence that your trustworthiness is taking hold. As your child moves into the unknown with ever more confident steps in the spiritual environment you strive to create, you will know that her hope in the Lord, too, is growing, step by step.

Becoming Independent

Sometime during the second year of life the child begins to move on to the second stage in the development of relationships. Trust is no longer the primary issue. Instead, now it becomes autonomy. You know you've reached that stage when your formerly compliant child begins to respond to you with a resounding "No!" Your child begins to indicate in large and small ways that she has her own ideas. Your sweet little thing makes her own declaration of independence. Enter "the terrible twos," as this time unfortunately has been labeled.

Your child's early attempts at independence—autonomy—may appear to be cute, even humorous. But as these cute incidents go on week after week and soon for months, they are no longer cute. "What happened to my baby?" you ask. You suspect that you're in for a long, tough struggle.

But even this struggle is an evidence of growth. Your child would not be *able* to move on to appropriate independence without a trustworthy environment.

But keep in mind that how you respond to your child's early probing at independence further influences the foundation of your child's concept of God. How do you react to a challenge of your authority? How do you feel about this emerging independence? How do you deal with "No!"?

Your responses will profoundly affect the way your child later pictures God's love and providential care. You can give your child the opportunity to test her decisions and her defiance. You can allow independence for the sake of learning. But you can also stand by to protect your fledgling from serious harm.

On the other hand, you could discourage these early attempts at independence. You could view the emergence of autonomy as a threat to your authority. You could continue firm control of your child's actions and learning.

God gave Adam and Eve the ability to make decisions—a free will. Yes, there was a risk. They could decide to do what He didn't want. And that they did, the Bible tells us. But God's response was not to restrict their free will in the daily affairs of life. They kept that.

He did, however, restrict their mobility, in a sense. He punished them by removing them from the Garden—permanently. But His love remained constant. Their attempts at independence were punished just as God had warned. But they were disciplined with love, with constancy, and with a continuation of His care. While rejecting and punishing the *sin*, God still accepted and loved them, though *sinners*!

Remember, your responses to your child's budding independence are shaping the foundations of her concept of God and how He deals with His people. Your relationship with your child now becomes a root that can produce a full-grown understanding of God and of mankind's role in God's world.

Faith Development

Your child's faith is not—nor can it be—as complex as your own or that of another adult. Yet God values the faith of a child. He tells us so. Jesus directed the disciples to let the little children come to Him—even the very little children. He praised the faith of a little child, telling His disciples that they needed a faith like that of a little child in order to enter the kingdom of heaven (Matt. 18:3).

In one sense, we ought not speak of faith as "development" because the faltering, unsophisticated faith of a young child or a new Christian is truly saving *faith*. Such new faith is simple, yet ready to grow and *develop* through a journey of life experiences—ready to mature and flourish through a personal walk with the Lord—ready to deepen and *develop* through an increased understanding of God's *faith*fulness.

Your little child can have faith. The faith of your little child is valuable. It is important. Value it, watch it grow. Help it grow. Look for the unseen *right from the start*.

CHAPTER SEVEN

Outside of Eden

During those early weeks of new-parent euphoria, it never occurs to you that there might be trouble brewing in your Garden of Eden. Your new baby looks so cute—so sweet—so innocent.

Wait a minute! What happened to the sinful nature with which each person since Adam and Eve presumably has been born? It's hard to believe, isn't it? Looking at your own little "Adam" or "Sarah," you just don't see sin lurking around the corner, do you?

But none of us is perfect. That's just the way it is. "Christians aren't perfect—just forgiven," the popular bumper sticker reads. And babies aren't exempt. Waiting to break into your paradise, that sinful nature is there.

How will *you* respond to it? How has *God* responded to us? With anger? Yes, briefly. With rejection? No, not really. Love? Yes! Patience? Yes! Guidance? Yes! Can we respond any differently?

As your child grows and begins to explore the world, first on all fours and then on those two wobbly legs, you find a new problem arising. It has many names: misbehavior—getting into trouble—discipline—setting limits—discipline and discipling.

Misbehavior

Let's start with misbehavior. Even the word implies that some standards have been set. You set the standards and articulate the expectations. But your standards and expectations may not be realistic. Your baby may have difficulty living up to them.

What do you expect of your baby—of yourself? Can you expect too much? Very definitely.

As soon as your baby no longer stays where you put him, trouble begins. You have to start saying no. You have to set limits. You have to decide just what those limits will be—for you and for your baby.

Child-Proofing the World

Let's talk about setting limits. As long as your baby was immobile, the limits were physically determined—by the crib, the bassinet, the blanket on the floor, the car seat, the swing. Wherever you put her, she stayed.

Now, all of a sudden, she's crawling and reaching, pulling herself up on the furniture. Soon she'll be walking. Suddenly you have to worry about her safety—and your sanity. You have to begin to child-proof your home. You begin by looking at the world from a 27-inch vantage point. You ask yourself, "What does *she* see? Will she get hurt?" You also need to decide whether you can tolerate the mess she'll make and whether the imminent danger to your precious bric-a-brac is worth the stress on both of you.

In my opinion, there's one basic rule: If it's dangerous or too messy or too expensive for you to tolerate the watchfulness that is required, move it. Put it out of reach. Store it away. Lock it up. Don't leave anything where it can *cause* hurt or *be* hurt.

Every child between 18 and 24 months becomes The Great Explorer as everything comes off shelves and out of cabinets. Then they begin to climb, and your 27-inch guideline no longer applies. Almost nothing is out of reach, unless it's behind a door they can't open.

Now what? You have no out-of-reach places left. You now need two homes, one for living (how bare!) and one for storing everything. Since that's not realistic, we'll have to come up with a better solution. Let's get back to the idea of setting limits. Somewhere during these first two years, you'll have to begin to say no—and mean it! That's the hard part—saying it only when you really mean it.

During early infancy when those physical limits were

enough, life was basically serene. Now, suddenly, there's no guarantee. She rolls over and crawls off the blanket, heading straight for the potted plant by the window. She pulls herself up and walks along the furniture, right toward the glass dish on the coffee table. She's walking and comes into the kitchen, making a beeline for her favorite cabinet under the sink.

At first even that's easy. You just move things. But finally there's a point at which that's not possible. You say no instead. Your verbal no begins to replace the limits of the crib, the blanket, the closed door. Your no becomes the barrier. The problem and the goal are remembering to say no each and every time for the same reason, and to be as consistent and predictable as the sides of the crib, the edge of the blanket, and the closed door. Too often your verbal limits *move* and your toddler wonders, "Will she say 'NO!' this time? How much can I do today? How big a mess will she tolerate today?"

Misbehavior and Forgiveness

Wait a minute! What does limit-setting have to do with your child's faith development? Plenty. How you set limits and deal with misbehavior creates a picture of how God deals with us. Your child is much too young to understand that, but she's building a storehouse of concepts and expectations. Her concept of how God deals with sin and offers forgiveness begins with how you treat her. Are you consistent? Are you fair? Predictable? Loving and forgiving? Only as she experiences those relationships through you, can she begin to understand how a loving and forgiving God deals with her.

Realistic Expectations

How you decide which issue to confront and which to avoid for now is equally important. Some behaviors are worth a fight. But some expectations are too sophisticated *at this time* to be worth the effort they will require.

My friend's daughter, Susan, was one year old when her brother Ben was born—probably not ideal in terms of optimal child development for either of them, but there they were. All survived nicely until Ben was ready to crawl. Susan had had the kitchen and family room to herself since she had learned to walk about eight months earlier. She was a curious, independent, but obedient young traveler. *No* had been quite easily established so far without major confrontations.

Those were the days before playpens had lost their favor, and a beautiful wood version graced my friend's family room. Ben spent some of his waking hours inside it, partly for his own protection. There he could play without having toys taken away by Big Sister. That, however, didn't work when he began to show interest in crawling. Crawling takes room. It requires floor space. It demands something to reach for, to crawl toward. Ben *had* to be out on the floor.

So out on the floor he went. Simple? Definitely not! The minute Ben began to get up on all fours and tried to figure out how to move those arms and legs to get somewhere, there was Susan. "Giddyap," she'd say and climb on his back.

Susan and her daddy had been having a game of horsy almost every night. Daddy cooperated very well, and Susan loved it. "Giddyap" was the magic word that led to exciting adventures, traveling all around the room.

When Ben began to try out that horsy position, there was only one thing for Susan to do—and only one thing Ben could do, too. He would plop down in utter frustration and cry.

My friend's first solution was to say no to Susan. But as she thought about it, that wouldn't really work. How could she explain to an 18-month-old that her favorite game was off limits with her brother but still okay with Dad? Even if she could explain, was it worth the effort? How much time would it take? How much frustration would it cause for Ben? Too much, she decided.

She needed another solution: Ben needed to learn to

crawl; for that he needed floor space. Susan needed to leave him alone; Ben had enough frustration without her demands. Mom needed to be with both of them; putting Susan in another room was out of the question; she wouldn't stay there anyway.

The playpen! It had been Ben's refuge from Big Sister. Could it now become Susan's territory to protect Ben? It was worth a try. In Susan went, complete with books, toys, and even a snack.

Susan wasn't particularly happy with the arrangement. She hadn't been confined to nine square feet of space in months. She didn't have to be. But using the sides of the playpen to say no to her favorite game for a few days was much easier on Mom than the constant surveillance her verbal no would have required. More important, Ben had been showing signs of giving up crawling if it meant dealing with Susan. He wouldn't even try when she was on the floor nearby.

My friend chose not to make this an issue with Susan because she felt it was too complex for Susan's cognitive understanding. I'm not sure that she as a young mother could have analyzed it clearly, but she intuitively found a clear and workable solution that responded to the developmental needs of Ben without burdening Susan with demands and explanations she could not understand.

You, too, will find issues not worth confronting. You will explore and find alternative solutions. Removing the problem removes the need for confrontation. It allows you to concentrate on only one or two nos at a time.

Yes and No

Your child needs to hear *yes* as well as *no*—and *yes* far more frequently than *no*. Think about the Garden of Eden. God gave Adam and Eve a large, lovely garden for their use. And He gave them one no. They had one tree from which they were not to eat. A whole garden full of *yeses*, but only one *no!* Your child's world needs to be like that—filled with *yes* and *no*, but with limited amounts of *no*. Like Adam and Eve, your child will find that no! That's a part of our legacy from our first parents—sin. We are all sinful. So like God, you need to mean "No" when you say it, and to follow up your words with action.

But you need to say no in a loving way. True, God removed Adam and Eve from the garden, but He did give them a second chance. His love prompted the promise of a Savior and the promise of forgiveness. Though He rejected what Adam and Eve had done, He still loved them. He hated the sin, but still loved His creation, the sinner. Today, as then, the sinner who does not reject His love and forgiveness has nothing to fear.

Discipline

Parents need to recognize the sin-legacy, the tendency to rebel and turn against the will of God and the laws of man. That inherited tendency makes our children misbehave, sometimes intentionally. That's the nature of mankind. If we as parents respond properly to that misbehavior, that sin, it will give our children a true glimpse of God. Do they see love and forgiveness? Do they see acceptance of themselves as *persons* in spite of wrong *actions*? Do they experience an environment filled with interesting and appropriate things to explore, provided just for them?

Though you live outside of Eden, given an understanding of child behavior and a Christian view of it, children's problems are manageable. Even the word *discipline* gives you a clue. Take a look!

Discipline—Discipling

Only one letter has changed *discipline* to *discipling*— e to g. In a musical scale, from e to g would be two steps— one small, one large.

We can also think of discipline as having two steps as we move from discipline to discipling. One small step is called *attitude* or *expectations*, which requires getting yourself ready for your child's mobility. The large step is called *environment-management* or *child-proofing*. You need to get your "garden" ready for your child's mobility.

Let's step over to *discipling*. It means "making followers, teaching, training, or leading in the correct path." But that's what *discipline* really is, isn't it? True discipline includes leading in the correct path—teaching, training, making followers. That is really our goal in disciplining children: making followers who will go down the correct behavioral path.

Discipline and *disciple* have the same Latin root. *Discipulus* is the Latin word for *pupil*. *Disciplina* means *teaching* or *instruction*. A disciple is one who is disciplined, that is, taught. Note what a positive meaning is intended.

Making a Disciple

The writer of the book of Proverbs says it so well: "Train a child in the way he should go. . . ." (Prov. 22:6). "The way he should go" implies also behavioral expectations.

Jesus said it beautifully as He was about to leave His disciples on the Mount of Olives: "Go and make disciples of all nations . . . and teach them to obey everything I have commanded you" (Matt. 28:19–20). "Teach them to obey" has the same ring to it as the Proverbs passage. For very young children the first way to make disciples is to establish behavioral expectations, to provide much the same kind of predictable environment outside of Eden as our first parents had in the garden—that is, repeated opportunities for choosing right behavior. Because of the fall into sin, that must include a forgiving, loving, and accepting environment.

Acceptance and Personality

We accept (sometimes with difficulty) the child's explorations of his rapidly expanding world. We accept (sometimes with reluctance) each child's style of exploration. Your child's personality will powerfully affect how she attacks the world and her experiences in it. Some children are happy and outgoing, inviting each new experience with zest and enthusiasm. Some children are timid and tentative, approaching new experiences and an expanding world from the safe distance of Mom's or Dad's lap. Some children are combative and challenging, testing each new opportunity with questions, determination, and an insatiable desire to win. Right or wrong is usually not the issue for these children. The tempting and challenging are almost always foremost considerations. Compliance is not easy for the combative child.

We do not form the personality for our children. Some researchers say that major personality traits of the newborn can be identified at seven days. Your child's personality determines how you approach the task of discipling. Compared with the combative, challenging child, the timid, tentative child will need yes far more often than no.

As you get to know your new baby, you will begin to respond in ways exactly right for *this* child. Your responses and the limits set will provide just the right environment to train up this child in the way the Lord expects.

Glimpses of God

Giving your child a glimpse of God through your responses and interactions with her will set the stage for the child's understanding of God's love and forgiveness.

You can never *fully* model God's love and forgiveness. However, you can, with the Holy Spirit's help, show your child glimpses of God's love and forgiveness. Life outside of Eden *can* encourage and build for your child a positive relationship with a loving, forgiving God—*right from the start!*

BUILDING
RELATIONSHIPS

CHAPTER EIGHT

The Silent Witness

Your child appropriates values based on what is important to you. As parents you are the most significant persons in your child's life. You provide food, warmth, and love, but also values.

Values, however, are provided in a different manner from food and warmth or even love. Values for the young child are absorbed through daily experiences that silently reflect your standards by what is chosen or not chosen, done and not done, said and not said. Little by little, children learn what you value and begin to absorb and adopt those same standards.

Valuing faith in Jesus and its meaning for life—for trust and prayer, for example—is important to the Christian parent. Only if you personally regard faith highly and appreciate what it does for you, can you impart the message that faith is important for your child. The child gets the message as you demonstrate faith's value in your own daily life. The child's understanding grows as you share and live your faith naturally.

Faith in Action

Perhaps it will be easier to understand the power of faith in action by an example where faith is absent. A Sunday school teacher was thanked recently for contributing to Alexis' faith life. "Oh," said the teacher, "I had no idea that I had made such an impact. What do you mean?" The mother went on to describe how she was beginning to see that, for Alexis, trusting God was becoming a natural part of living.

One evening at dusk Mom and Alexis were at home when a severe thunderstorm broke, just when Dad was en route home from work. Mom silently worried, "With all that traffic and the low visibility, Sam could be in an accident." Alexis prayed aloud, "Dear Jesus, please keep Daddy safe in this storm."

Mom stopped short. Alexis' first thought and action was one of prayer. Her own had been one of worry. Alexis was openly and innocently demonstrating that faith was becoming important to her—a value that she was learning in Sunday school.

Faith became important to Mom, too, in later months through the genuine, sometimes silent, witness that flowed from her young daughter's budding trust in God. Mom's faith grew through the unspoken but resounding witness of Alexis' faith.

How fortunate for Alexis and her family that her Sunday school teacher brought the witness of the Word. How sad for Alexis and her family that the witness came only in Sunday school, not day by day at home.

Your new baby or toddler can see the Gospel, God's good news of forgiveness and salvation, long before Sunday school. She can "hear" the Gospel through the silent but resounding witness of your life and walk with God. She has the chance to hear the not-so-silent Gospel through prayers, conversations, and Bible stories.

Sharing Your Faith

Do you share your faith with your child? Does your young child have any clues that you walk and talk with God on a daily basis? Your child should see that, for you—as for Alexis—faith is a normal and natural part of life. Your child should come to understand that trusting God is as natural and regular in your life as breathing.

How can you provide those clues? What will communicate the silent witness of your faith? How much of the silent witness is not so silent after all?

Considerable evidence confirms that the values absorbed in the home during a child's first three years of life powerfully influence the value system far into adulthood. Daily experiences that signal values—what is important—mold and shape how the child thinks. They very much determine how the child—and the later adult—makes decisions and sets priorities.

Setting priorities for demonstrating your own faith—the ways in which you manifest your relationship with your Lord—conveys an unspoken gospel to your child. You demonstrate your faith in the Gospel when you establish daily routines and times for communicating with God through study of the Bible. Through the Word, the Holy Spirit maintains and strengthens your faith. Now is the time to examine those priorities to be sure that they are what you want your child to assimilate during the growing years.

Prayers

Pray without ceasing—pray continuously—is the guideline given to us by St. Paul (1 Thess. 5:17). Like Alexis, yours can be a life of prayer. You, like Alexis, can choose to pray before worrying. Many Christians do. But signaling your prayer life to your family is more challenging. Does your spouse know about it? Does your child catch clues that you converse with God regularly? Check whether you are sending meaningful signals.

I used to pray quietly in my heart over my children while I diapered them. I also talked and cooed with them as they lay there and enjoyed getting dry again. But seldom did I think of speaking a prayer aloud. Sharing prayer with Diane, Dan, or Lynelle—as well as the gagas and goo-goos—was an opportunity that I missed!

Don't miss it with your child. She can't know about your prayers unless you verbalize them. She won't feel that your conversation with God is natural and frequent unless she hears it. Pray aloud throughout the day to provide the evidence that will give your child a glimpse of your faith.

Just as important, you can and should also share God's answers to your prayers. Do your clues unintentionally suggest that prayer exists in a vacuum? You can talk about God's answers to your prayers. You should communicate that the answer isn't always *yes*. Sometimes God says *no* or *wait*.

If children learn communication—conversation—between people by hearing it, how much more important to learn communication with God by hearing. If a child develops conversation skills by hearing conversation and participating in it, the same principle can be applied to prayer—conversation with God!

Don't expect your child to grasp the meanings and messages of these conversations right from the start. But you can expect that she will begin to grasp the importance, purpose, and expectations of an active, natural, and continuous prayer relationship with a very real God.

Your Personal Walk

You should also examine your personal quiet time—the time spent alone with your Lord for Bible reading, prayer, and meditation. No, I'm not suggesting that you share your time for quiet meditation with a restless, rambunctious toddler! But your personal quiet time is a part of that silent Gospel witness I referred to earlier. Your time with the Lord will spill over later into the rest of your day. Unnoticed and without specific intention, your faith shows in numerous ways and in turn colors your activities throughout the day.

When my daughter Lynelle was in high school, she said casually one day that she could see that my faith was growing and deepening. Surprised by her comment, I asked her how she could tell. She replied that she knew I was spending more time each day in personal quiet time and that probably meant something was happening in my faith life.

Incidentally, she was right. Although my quiet time—like that of most mothers—was carved out of early morning or late evening hours (sometimes both), she noticed. Though by definition quiet time means being alone with God, your family reads the evidence. The evidence could be the stack of books beside the chair you've set aside for your talks with God, the open Bible on the coffee table that changes positions each day it is used, or an attitude of prayer that grows out of the time spent alone with God.

For new parents, maintaining such private time with God is a challenge. The predictable pieces of time from which it can be carved seem to be rare and precious. You may have to settle for the unpredictable and snatch your quiet time from various parts of the day when your baby is sleeping or playing contentedly in her crib. But you do need to commit yourself to find time to meditate each day on His Word.

The Community of Believers

You also need to continue family devotions—or begin them if they aren't already a daily routine. Whether you are a family of three or thirteen, time together with God is important. Time together should include devotional materials, songs, and whatever will help all members of the family grow.

Gradually the newest member of the family will join your time together. As she grows into the routine of family study, worship, and prayer, she can begin to participate in ways that are meaningful to her, kept simple to match her level of understanding. Membership and experience in a family of believers will influence her life patterns profoundly as she begins to build her own walk with God.

Give her your silent witness. Share your witness silently through your daily life, and you will be witnessing resoundingly to your faith. Share that witness aloud through your family devotions, your spontaneous prayers, your praise of God, and your comments about answered prayer. Give her a worthwhile model. Provide that witness—starting today—*right from the start!*

CHAPTER NINE

A Legacy of Love

Having a child profoundly changes your life as a married couple. It may be twenty years before you'll be "just a couple" again. That's an awesome thought, isn't it?

Even more sobering is that, according to current divorce statistics, all of you will not make it through the next twenty years as couples, though most of you will beat the statistics if you are committed to marriage and family—*your* marriage and family.

Marriage takes commitment, love, time, and hard work. The most powerful way to describe and depict love for your growing child is to bring to the relationship with your spouse a generous amount of love, commitment, time, and hard work.

Living Love

The New Testament frequently speaks of faith and love at the same time. In his letter to the Corinthian Christians, Paul says that faith, hope and love remain, but the greatest of the three is love (1 Cor. 13:13). Why is love so important? How can it be more important than faith?

True, faith will not be necessary in the hereafter because we will be with God. But beyond that, God's love is basic to our faith. It activates our faith. We love Him because He first loved us (1 John 4:19). We *can* love only because He first loved us. Our love is a response to His redeeming love and is possible through the faith that we have in Jesus as our Savior. Our love flows from our faith in Jesus Christ.

Your love for your spouse (and for all others) is enhanced by your love for the Lord. That doesn't mean there are no problems in your marriage. It doesn't mean you'll never disagree. But Jesus' love will become a model for forgiveness and a reason to forgive. Love and forgiveness together create the glue that will keep your marriage relationship strong. Pass that glue!

Creating the Glue Formula

By the time you become parents, you have discovered that marriage involves negotiation. To live "happily ever after" is impossible. To live as happily as is possible takes hard work! Love is a verb, an action. Love isn't something that happens to you; it's something you do—every day. Your commitment to each other is based on your continuous thoughts and actions. It involves forgiveness of misunderstandings, harsh words, actions, and inactions. That takes communication. Add a lot of communication to the glue formula.

Some young couples are surprised, even distressed to discover how much hard work is involved in a marriage. They expected success to be natural and they haven't recovered from their starry-eyed expectations before the wedding ceremony. Maybe, they reason, a baby will help. A baby will make us a real family. A baby will be proof of our love and will keep us together—and happy. A baby is the glue we need for this marriage.

Will the Glue Hold?

But no baby can or should be expected to be the glue. No baby asks to take on the job of solving the parents' problems. In actual fact, adding a baby often strains rather than strengthens the relationship of a couple. The strain of childbirth itself can be serious.

To be sure, the arrival of your first child is exciting. You think you're prepared for the physical care required for a virtually helpless infant. You expect it will mean sleepless nights and busy days. You can guess it will mean abruptly restricting your social life, at least for a while.

But what you're not prepared for is the strain this infant can bring to your marriage.

Jealousy, misunderstandings, and loss of intimacy enter with a rude shock. No one told you it would be like this. And if someone had, you would have regarded the warning as preposterous.

But this is real. Many a new father feels twinges of jealousy when his wife begins to spend almost all her time with the baby. He knows she is busy being a new mother but he feels ignored. And he adds to the problem by keeping his emotions to himself, secretly admitting guilt: "I shouldn't feel this way, but I do!" And the new mother is so consumed, so infatuated with her new responsibilities in those early weeks, that she doesn't even realize what is happening to Dad. She is too busy, too tired, to be sensitive or to read his reactions the way she always did before the baby. Feeling ignored and at the same time guilty for giving in to his selfish thoughts, he, too, tries to ignore.

Soon many a new mother feels trapped, overwhelmed by the unending round of tasks to be performed and by their unending sameness. After the first weeks, exciting because it's all so new, time moves on—wears on—and the newness wears off. Enter the after-baby loneliness, the post-partum blues, the realization that this state of affairs is irrevocable! Mom believes she's lost everything—her shape, her contact with the outside world, and her ability to communicate intelligently with her childless friends.

She often senses that her husband doesn't understand these new feelings of self-doubt. Maybe she hasn't even shared her feelings with Dad because they're so different from her before-baby emotions. Though she hasn't voiced these gnawing feelings, many a new mom feels unloved, unappreciated, and alone because her husband isn't responding to her unspoken needs.

Straining the Bond

In addition, both parents often feel betrayed by a loss

of privacy and intimacy which this new intruder has created. Their time alone for each other just isn't any more. Even their lovemaking can no longer be spontaneous. It has to fit in around feeding, diapering, and sleeping schedules. Even when baby is safely tucked in and sound asleep, Mom makes love with one ear on the crib, ready to stop if baby starts crying. How unromantic!

But wait! That's not all. Predictability has gone out the window, too. On many days chaos is all that can be predicted. Suppose a new mom and dad were used to going out to brunch after church on Sundays. Suppose they often took long walks together in the evening. Suppose they enjoyed impromptu visits to museums or art galleries or even shopping malls. Suddenly spur-of-the-moment decisions are out of the question. Formerly comfortable routines are now so bogged down with preparation and paraphernalia that they hardly seem worth the effort.

Added to the loss of routine is a loss of those times set aside just to talk, to really communicate. Dinner is sandwiched between feedings. Long walks are long gone. Late night talks are shortened so that Mom can get some sleep before the next feeding. Both parents feel cheated because their formerly favorite activities and chatting sessions are now so burdened with babyness.

Or maybe your challenge grows totally out of the newness of being a parent team. Until now maybe your separate careers and busy lives have given you little time or reason to work together. Oh, you've always had time for each other. That's not the problem. But what a shock to your security and stability to find you now need to plan ahead, to check with each other before making commitments that must be worked out cooperatively with baby *and* spouse in mind! The burden of babyness is bigger because it seems like the first time you have needed to think and work as a team—though you should have been doing it all along!

Do you see yourself in any of these scenarios? Take heart if you do. You're normal! But you needn't accept the "normal" without a fight. You can combat the after-baby-marriage syndrome.

Forging a Permanent Bond

You're no longer just a wife or a husband. Suddenly you're a wife-and-mother, a husband-and-father. The titles bring new roles, new responsibilities, new stresses. The first step toward relieving the stress is to recognize it. Talk about it! Openly air your feelings of frustration, of jealousy, of neglect! Feelings are very real, even when you think they are baseless.

The second step is to take action. Do something constructive about the stresses. Find ways to help Dad feel less jealous, less ignored. Find ways to diminish Mom's feelings of loneliness, of being trapped. Plan strategies to regain and enjoy intimacy. Create ways to reinstate favorite routines, probably with a new twist.

Strengthening the Glue

The overall solution to the problems of after—baby—marriage syndrome can be stated simply: Make time to be together—time spent regularly and predictably alone together! That means time without baby—with no interruptions—no distractions. The tricky part of the solution is finding that time for your particular case.

You will be able to do it if you are convinced that it is absolutely essential—if you are willing to make that time a priority—if you understand that a part of being a good mother is being a good wife—or that part of being a good father is being a good husband.

Set aside time each week. Make a date with each other. Get a babysitter and go for a walk, go bike riding, go out to dinner. Even a nursing baby can survive without Mom for an hour or so. You'll come back refreshed and ready for another week of all-consuming routine. For budget-minded parents, hiring a sitter for something as mundane as a walk around the block may seem outrageously extravagant, but isn't your marriage worth the investment?

Set aside time each day—time to talk together, to

pray together, to laugh together. Get up 15 minutes earlier and sit together over coffee or tea before the baby wakes up. Stay up 15 minutes later and chat over a glass of lemonade or a cup of tea. Snatch those 15 minutes when Dad comes home from work. Dinner can wait. Have a cup of coffee or fruit juice together first. Then finish the meal preparation together.

As soon as Mom is ready, set aside time for love-making. Tune in to each other. If you're afraid of disturbing the baby, or of being disturbed by her, find a symphony or a love song on the radio to block out the distraction. Learn to let the baby whimper for a few minutes rather than interrupt this time together. Your love made you parents in the first place. Don't neglect that closeness so long that it has to be rebuilt again after a year or more of drifting!

Set aside time for all three of you to establish new routines, too. If the distance permits, a brief excursion to the park, to a museum, to a shopping mall, to the nearest woods, or to the beach—all are manageable with a stroller or baby-pack, some extra diapers, a bottle of water or juice, and a pacifier. Learn to travel light and to keep a diaper bag packed so that nearly-impromptu events are still possible.

Love Is Action

Love is not just a feeling. It is a commitment, a decision to love each other, to "be" in love, to *stay* in love by working at your commitment. It means keeping the feelings of love alive by *showing* love.

Your acts of love—with each other, with your baby—are a mirror of God's love. Your child begins to understand love and learns to love in return by being loved and by seeing love in action. Your child learns to love by being loved first and thereby catches a glimpse of God's love upon seeing love in action in each of you.

Glimpsing God's Love

If your love is to reflect God's love, you must try to understand His love. You must begin to comprehend its constancy and consistency. Only then will you be able to help your child experience God's love through you.

But can we understand God's love? What are the qualities that make His love so unique? How do we model God's love through our love? God's love is special. Can ours be that special? Of course not, but we can attempt to approximate His love if we contemplate the unique qualities of it.

God's love is unconditional. It's there for us whether we accept it or not. Remember, He loved us first by sending His only Son Jesus who lived the perfect life in our place and paid the price for our sin. There are no strings attached—no ifs, no buts. He loves us in spite of our sin and waywardness. He loves us even when we do not love in return. We may try to add conditions, hoping to make His love more comprehensible, hoping to comprehend the incomprehensible (Rom. 11:33–36). Any conditions are ours, not God's.

Like an underground stream, God's love is there whether we tap into it or not. Only if we draw from it, can we taste it, drink of its depths, and quench our thirst. It becomes an access well of faith built for us by God Himself! We only decide how deeply we will drink.

God's love is consistent, always there, always the same, always complete. God's love cannot be once hot, once cold, once in, then out. Unlike us, God does not withhold His love because of anger. He does not weaken; He never tires. He never ignores us because of preoccupation; He never delays because of other more pressing tasks.

Unlike ours, God's love is consistent, like a rock that can't be moved or change. God is always there, stable in spite of our instability— always predictable despite our unpredictability. God is always there with His offer of forgiveness, even when we are too angry to accept forgiveness, too busy to remember forgiveness, or too preoccupied to appreciate forgiveness.

God's love is unending, eternal. He doesn't decide to turn it off one day and on the next. He doesn't lose interest. He doesn't fall out of love. His is an active, committed love—a permanent commitment—with each one of us. With God, love really *is* forever!

Incomprehensible Love

God sees forever even when we can't. He accepts forever even though we don't. He loves forever in spite of our failings. God's love is forever—unending—permanent—eternal!

How challenging to contemplate an incomprehensible God loving us into an unending, incomprehensible eternity! Our finite human nature can never fully grasp that. And yet we try—must try.

The circle of God's love is without beginning and without end—complete and perfect. The circle of *our* love is made complete in Christ as it reaches out to embrace others—husbands—wives—children—your baby.

As you live in God's love and experience it, you show love to others. And so you make God's incomprehensible love a little more comprehensible to others. Through you, God's love becomes real to your spouse and to your child.

Living God's Love

Your relationship with God speaks to your child long before the words are understandable, based on God's unconditional, constant, eternal love. Your relationship with your child can mirror that God-relationship growing out of experiences thoughtfully built upon your own relations with her, as well as through the Biblical words of faith she begins to hear from her parents.

Each of us has a God-concept based in part on the understanding of power, authority, and love formed during our early years with our own parents. Ours is an image of a loving God if we have experienced parental love and God's love as young children. We can grasp some understanding of God's consistent and unconditional love if we have experienced such love in our relationships with adults, especially with our parents. Conversely, we form a concept of a convicting and capricious God if the important adult authority in our lives has been punitive and capricious. If we experienced neglect, disinterest, or even abuse from the significant adults in our childhood, that became the foundation for a skewed, unscriptural God-concept.

As an adult and a new parent, you need to understand the power and the role of love in those early experiences—with and without love. You need to be aware of the potential influence on your child's concepts of God's love. Awareness will help you monitor the messages you send your new baby. They should be messages of love that is unconditional, consistent, and permanent.

A tall order—an awesome, almost frightening divine prescription! Your power to fill it, however, is not within yourself. It comes from God as you relate to His love and forgiveness. Christ's death and resurrection make it possible to have a relationship with God. That relationship and your daily experience of it give you the power to show love to your growing child. It ensures for your child a legacy of God's love coming through you—from God, through the love in your marriage.

This legacy is based on actions that grow out of love and demonstrate it. Unconditional love offers forgiveness. Consistent love includes predictability. Unending love provides permanence.

As the Holy Spirit leads you through the Word to show love by means of the Gospel, strive to make forgiveness, predictability, and stability a part of *your* love for each other and of your love together for your child. Give *your* child a legacy of love. Pass the glue of love. Make it a permanently bonding glue—*right from the start.*

CHAPTER TEN

Walking the Way

Very early in your adventure as a new parent you will want to set priorities. Priority-setting is especially important in deciding how you will spend the time away from your workplace. Whether your workplace is in the home or an hour's commute away (on a good day!), you will need to learn how and where to find enough time for your new responsibility and joy (read baby).

Setting Priorities

How you spend your "disposable time" becomes of utmost importance right from the start. The patterns set during the first year of your child's life will usually be the ones you follow all through your child's growing years. The way you plan and apportion the pieces of your day will govern the way you think about yourself and your family.

When your baby is brand new, you readily find time for this fascinating and responsive bundle of smiles and kicks. You eagerly spend a few minutes here and there cooing and gurgling with such an appreciative audience. Almost any time of the day will do, because there are a few minutes here and there at all hours when the baby is up, awake, and alert. You won't even have to think about adapting your own schedule to the baby's for at least several weeks.

Quality Time

At the beginning, all the time you spend with your baby will be "quality time." "This isn't so hard," you say to yourself. "What's all the fuss about quality time? All the time I spend with my baby is quality time!"

But slowly things begin to change. Dad or Mom finds that when they come home from work a few minutes late, the baby isn't always responsive to their funny faces—in fact, sometimes is downright fussy! So Mom or the sitter puts the baby to bed a few minutes earlier the next day to avoid the fussiness. Before you realize what has happened, the child is often asleep before you get home, and maybe even asleep when you leave in the morning.

But suppose that Mom has decided to stay home for the next year or so and be a full-time parent. After all, that's what's best for the baby, isn't it?

That's it! We'll do whatever is best for the baby. So you write a letter of resignation and prepare to live happily ever after among the diapers, toys, and baby.

So now *all* your time is spent with baby. Or is it? Somebody has to make the meals, wash the baby clothes, and cook the beds. (Or is it cook the meals and make the beds?—you're getting weary and confused.) *Somebody* has to keep the household running smoothly.

Soon you find yourself doing some of the chores that used to be on Dad's list (before he was "Dad," of course). Then you find that three hours of unbroken sleep between feedings isn't exactly a good night's sleep—you get the picture! Being a full-time mom doesn't mean it's all focused on the baby after all. There goes "quality time"— right out the window.

Being Available

Both of you, Mother and Father, find yourselves having to snatch time to do things you used to take for granted—like sitting down for a leisurely cup of coffee after dinner—like running the countless errands that won't wait—like planning a quiet evening together without interruptions.

That's it! That's what life has become! Interruptions! Ever since you brought the baby home from the hospital, life has become an endless string of interruptions. If you're really honest with yourselves, at times you even resent all those interruptions.

But you're not honest with yourselves. And you're certainly not honest with each other. It's hard to admit that there are even times when, after all, you're not so sure about this parent business. What seemed like a good idea a year ago has turned into a 20-year-long interruption!

Oops! Did I really write that? How could anyone long for the good old pre-baby days? At least, how could anyone admit it?

It's About Time

Finding time. That's what this chapter is about. Finding time for your baby—for each other—for yourself—for all the mundane necessities of life. Finding time becomes a preoccupation, and that makes things even worse!

So you need to set priorities. You need to decide what is important and what is expendable—or, as a minimum, what can be abbreviated a little. Life becomes a barrel of complex choices. Finding a sensible and caring way to sort out the choices can defy the best.

Quality vs. Quantity Time

There's only so much time in each day, right? So all you have to do is figure out how to convert quantity into quality for everyone concerned. You've read the articles touting "quality time," as opposed to quantity, as the sensible goal for the busy parent. The *kind* of time—the *quality* of time—you spend with your baby is more important than the amount—quality versus quantity. Sounds reasonable? Yes and no. Quality time *is* important, to be sure. But so is the quantity.

As you struggle to set priorities for your new and busier life, you still have only the same, God-given, 24-hour day. The struggle now is to apportion (juggle!) that time wisely—to make sure there is time for God, for family (suddenly that has a new meaning, right?), for job, for relaxation.

Since every day is still only twenty-four hours long (even when they seem longer!), you have to learn to spend those hours in a way that honors God and supports your family. The mundane things are still necessary. But are there shortcuts?

Do you really have to vacuum every day? Can the kitchen tolerate a little loving neglect? Can those papers or journals or projects wait until tomorrow at work? Can the newspaper wait until the baby is asleep? Can you, the creature of habit, change your habits to reflect your new priorities? Can you develop some new, good habits, for example, to do certain things only once, to do them now, and save time in the long run?

In the same way, Dad and Mom can review their work and activity outside the home and make slight adjustments. Is every out-of-town trip really essential? Can you find a way to streamline your take-home work to cut down on the time it takes? Is there a way to be really *home* when you're home?

Many years ago, when I was the mother of one, and the expectant mother of another, as well as the "decorator and furnisher" of a new house, a carpeting salesman lectured me about raising a family, not a house. Although I still bought the gold carpeting I was considering (which he hinted broadly was too delicate for a growing family), I never forgot what he said.

"Your children will probably not remember whether the kitchen floor was always spotless," he said, "but they will remember whether you had time for them." Wise words from an unexpected source!

Intentional Attention

How do you get it all done and still find time for everything? That's the heart of the matter. Finding time isn't the answer. *Making time* is. You need to decide deliberately where you will focus your attention. You need to *make* time intentionally for your baby, whose schedule can't always fit yours. You need to adjust your timetable to fit your baby's, not vice versa.

You need to focus on the real heart of the matter—your *heart!*—and center on the relationship with your new baby, not on the tasks and trivialities of everyday life nor even on the demanding *physical* needs of your baby.

More important are this little bundle's smiles and wiggles and kicks. You need to enjoy and savor each new accomplishment and record it in your memory bank (and the baby book, of course) before this one makes way for the next accomplishment. You need to be there—really there—when you're there for your child. Your baby needs your active attention. You need to connect with your child in some nose-to-nose time.

That's what interaction really is—nose-to-nose, focused time with all eyes, ears, smiles, and nose involved with this little one who will grow up all too fast—though that seems impossible at the moment. Truly focused interaction leaves you at peace with yourself, even when the schedule gets changed or the floor stays dirty while you play and talk with your baby.

Intentional interaction brings peace though that extra journal doesn't get read and tonight's homework becomes tomorrow's office task. Attentive time allows you to focus on the spirit and feeling between you and your baby and to work on that relationship. That also means being dependably and predictably available to your child for that time.

When Diane and Dan were toddlers, they learned quickly that the first half hour that Daddy was home from work in the evening was play time—time to crawl on the floor, on Daddy and over Daddy—time to giggle and tickle and wriggle and squeal. It was *their* time. When Lynelle's needs were added to the pack, they had to make room for another giggler and wriggler. "The more, the merrier" was sometimes a little much for Dad, who was at the bottom of the heap for those adventures.

But how important that was for those toddlers as

they played with Dad! That laid the groundwork for later communication and interaction. But intentional attention takes time, work, and energy!

Interaction and time for the children aren't the only candidates for your attention. Someone really does have to cook the meals and make the beds! So you also have to figure out how to get done what needs to get done and still have time for your baby or toddler on the fly.

Walking the Way

That's it! On the fly! There has to be a way to do two things at once!—to do one thing while still giving that intentional attention to the other. Wouldn't it be nice if you really could raise your children on the fly?

I have good news for you. You can!

Several years ago, a researcher and theorist was interested in identifying family practices that produce what he called "competent young children" at age four or five. "Competent" was defined as one who was interested in the world around and confident enough to explore that world under the watchful eye of Mom or another adult. Hoping to discover the cause of *competence* and *less competence*, he arranged to videotape families with competent four-year-olds and those with less competent children of similar age.

Dr. Burton White and his associates came upon some interesting discoveries as they analyzed the tapes. The parents of competent youngsters all had a quality that the parents of less competent children lacked. He called it "on-the-fly parenting." He found that the parents who were, in fact, able to "do two things at once" and to respond to their children "on the fly" were rearing competent children! They had learned how to do two things at once!

"Aha," you say, "now there's a novel idea." Or is it?

Actually, God advocated and directed it way back in the Sinai Desert! Look at Deut. 6:6–7 where Moses explains how the Children of Israel were to teach their children and future generations the Ten Commandments which God had just given them.

First, the words were to be in their own hearts. We can only teach our children what we believe and what we ourselves consider important.

Secondly, they were to teach God's law diligently to their children. They were to make this teaching a high *priority* (sound familiar?) and to spend intentional time doing it.

But more, they were to "talk of them" when they sat in their houses. Each family had the responsibility. It could not be delegated. They were to talk about them early in the morning, walking along the way, going to bed at night, and getting up again in the morning. In other words, throughout the day parents had a responsibility to teach their children. Maybe "on the fly" isn't such a new idea after all!

Walking the way then becomes really walking God's way. Our job is to teach and give attention to our children, no matter what else we're also doing. "On the fly" is really God's idea in the first place. He gave us the idea, the directive, the commandment. And the Holy Spirit also gives us the wisdom and the ability to do it. Walk the way with your child, God's way, *right from the start.*

OUT AND BEYOND

CHAPTER ELEVEN

Great Expectations

Every night during my early childhood, my mother tucked me into bed. She'd sit on the bed while I said my prayers. Then we would sing a goodnight prayer together in German. As she turned out the light, she would say, "Good night. Sleep tight." And my younger sister would say in turn, "Don't let the bedbugs bite!" That little ritual was repeated over and over with the two of us, then also with my brothers and baby sister.

Years later, when I tucked my own children into bed, I found myself singing the same prayer, this time in English, and saying, "Good night. Sleep tight." I almost waited for my sister to say, "Don't let the bedbugs bite!" The ritual was in place.

I suspect that when my children have their own offspring to tuck into bed, they, too, will hear the parting wish, "Goodnight. Sleep tight!" By the way, those words *must* accompany turning out the lights. To say them sooner or later than that somehow isn't right.

I'm sure you find yourself repeating similar rituals from your own childhood. Each of you—mother *and* father—brought with you a storehouse of treasured rituals and expectations. You probably have not thought of them for years. But the new baby brings back the memories. In fact, you feel compelled to share these happy memories now with your own child.

Many of those treasured rituals are just that, having very little to do with right or wrong ways to raise children. But for you they carry emotions that go far beyond the actions themselves or even their meanings. They are a part of your personal storehouse of expectations for babyhood and childhood.

I'm sure that some of you simply had to buy a rocker

for your living room or nursery before your baby was born. Was this only because it would be a convenient place to hold and comfort your little one? Or was it because, even without putting it into words, you remembered being rocked as a baby? Was the rocker a necessary accessory for parenting rituals?

If it simply feels right to have a rocker for feeding, nursing, and cuddling your baby, chances are that feeling comes from your own childhood as a part of your "script" for parenting.

A Storehouse of Expectations

Each of us has a storehouse of memories—usually treasured ones—that we bring with us to adulthood and to the new task of parenting. Most of the memories in our deepest storehouse are so buried that it takes a baby to bring them back.

Ordinarily you don't have occasion to discuss them with your future spouse during courtship, nor can you explain them logically to another person. Often the most we can say is, This is the way we always did it.

Memories tend to become foundation stones for our own children, too, often unplanned, without any rational base, even without our being aware of them.

Building Expectations

The role of a parent—especially a parent of young children—is to build expectations. Parents need to fill the storehouse for the next generation. Stone by stone, we set in place the foundation for the expectations of living, the traditions, and the values.

A new house is built logically, step by step, beginning with the foundation before the walls or floors are added. For the more visible components, such as the windows and roof, to be straight and true, the unseen components below must be accurate.

The builder lays the foundation with the completed

building in mind. Without careful foundation work, all that comes after is harder and often fruitless.

Parents, too, build foundations or expectations of how things are to be done. These foundations support the walls of babyhood, the windows of childhood, and the doors of adulthood. For Christians, the Scriptures serve as the blueprint for the foundations, walls, windows, and doors.

Building Values

The adult superstructure of values rests on the foundations you build for the child. The childhood component values fit into a value system that is then used routinely—almost unconsciously—by the adolescent and adult.

Each of us builds a value system out of unconscious feelings and opinions that we hold "just because." What we value comes from experiences that have been important in our childhood. Our values in part come from what we observe to be important to the important people in our lives, especially parents and grandparents. We also value what comes from God's Word.

However, the critical process of value-building is often taken for granted or left to chance. Few of us think consciously or clearly how values are built experience by experience.

My young friend, Sharon, recently said, "I want Jessica to believe that prayer is important. I have decided to demonstrate its importance in my life by praying aloud and letting Jessica share my talking with God. I want her to catch a glimpse of the power of prayer as she observes my relationship with God."

Most Christians may feel that prayer is important, but they may not always be able to say why. Few new parents have thought about prayer as clearly as Sharon. The ritual of regular prayer becomes a block in the foundation of values that will be understood much later, a value system that Sharon and her husband, Peter, are helping Jessica build piece by piece. The ritual becomes habit, an expectation of what "always" happens.

Choosing the Blocks

A building that is strong and functional has been designed that way from the beginning by a good architect and executed by a skilled builder.

God has been the perfect architect for your child. Though His design for all of us was flawless, the world's first parents spoiled the plan. Since then we have all had to contend with inherent, inherited sin.

Our job as builders in the child's development is to provide the best materials, the best experiences, so that our "building" develops strength for the child of God. Our job is to choose the blocks of experience that will provide the foundation for our child's value system. Our job is to provide activities that will build expectations of a lasting and vital relationship with God.

So we need to think carefully about the kinds of experiences we build into our child's early years. Choosing the rituals which our children will later value is a major task of parenting.

The child already vaguely resembles the adult he or she will become. Yet much of what we do with and for this child during these first three years will profoundly affect the adult to come.

Building the Beginnings

As parents of a young child you have now the opportunity to decide consciously and clearly the expectations you want to build in your child—to see the Unseen (Jesus) and to build your child's expectations around this Friend. Through what you build, your child will become not only a part of your family, but also of God's family.

The expectations which you build will give direction and foundation for adulthood and a family of his or her own. Choose those expectations wisely and consciously so that the direction they give for the future will be pointed toward a real and personal relationship with a loving Savior. Choose those expectations with a clear view of the "expected end" in sight (Jer. 29:11).

Building the beginnings is always exciting. But what should they look like? If you were raised in a Christian home, look to your own memories for what you would like to pass on to the next generation. If you recently became a Christian, ask which new experiences and changing values should be transferred to your child.

Obviously you will want to include prayer, time with God in His Word, and an awareness of His presence throughout the day. The values and the adult you hope to see can easily be sketched. Realizing those hopes may be more challenging.

Beginnings

Begin at the beginning. Pray. Begin immediately. Pray with and for your child from the moment of birth. Pray aloud. Pray where your baby can hear your prayer.

Pray a child-size prayer over your child when you put him or her to bed, even for a nap. Use a hymn or prepared prayer to get started. Add a sentence or two, talking to God from your heart, but keep it simple enough for your child to grasp as the months go by.

Pray with your baby before meals and snacks. Again, choose words that a young child can understand. Encourage your child to join you in saying, "Thank You, Jesus" as soon as the words can be imitated. Begin with echo prayers (you say one or two words and your child repeats—echoes—the same words). Remind your child that praying is "talking to Jesus." Begin with only one name for God (Jesus is for many children the easiest because He became a real man for us). Use that name to pray at formally set times such as meals and bedtimes and also spontaneously throughout the day.

Share your own prayer life aloud with your child at least part of the time. But be sure that the ideas you share aloud are such that your child can grasp them. Many concerns that we share with God each day may frighten a little child rather than build a loving relationship.

Sing "Jesus songs" with and for your child regularly throughout the day. Songs such as "Jesus Loves Me, This I Know" and "My Best Friend Is Jesus" are good for a beginning. If you don't know them, ask a friend to teach them to you. Buy a children's album of Christian songs and sing along. Buy a book such as *Little Ones Sing Praise* and play the songs on a piano or guitar. Use records, tapes, and Christian radio.

Use your own favorite hymns as lullabies. My children were often rocked as infants to "I Am Jesus' Little Lamb," which had been one of my own favorites as a child. In fact, the only songs I used as lullabies besides familiar "Jesus songs" were a few well-known nursery rhymes. It will be no surprise to hear those same songs being sung to the next generation!

Buy "Jesus books" for your little child as soon as your baby shows an interest in sitting long enough to look at pictures. Don't expect a baby to sit for a story. At first choose books that have colorful and recognizable pictures to point to and talk about.

Begin with books that have thick cardboard or cloth pages. You'll find several choices in your local Christian book store. Select those you really like, because you'll be reading them and talking about the pictures countless times!

Select a time of the day for a regular "visit with Jesus" or devotion time. For your young child, this will be a talking-about-Jesus-time, to which you can gradually add Bible stories and devotional songs. Keep this time short enough to match your child's short attention span. Be sure to add prayers that your child can echo or actions your child can repeat. For the very young "Hooray, Jesus!" is a child-size way to praise God. As your child approaches age three, you will be ready to use a resource such as *Little Visits with Jesus* from Concordia Publishing House, St. Louis, MO.

Choose a favorite picture of Jesus for your child's room. Consider a picture of Jesus with young children. Talk about the picture with your child. Point out the cross.

Talk about it and other Christian pictures and symbols you have in your home.

Talk about Jesus throughout the day to help your child feel that He is very real to you. Such conversations will help your baby come to know and love Jesus just as you do. Pray spontaneously and aloud to give your child a real and meaningful experience of praying without ceasing.

Offer your child great expectations of a personal walk with the Lord. Share your own walk so that your child sees firsthand the power and presence of God, *right from the start.*

CHAPTER TWELVE

Branching Out

Now that you have begun to think of yourselves as a "real" family, you are probably also becoming more aware of families around you. Interactions of other parents with their children suddenly take on new meaning when you have personal experiences very much the same. You may even wonder how other families solve the inevitable dilemmas that come up from time to time.

If you are a part of a worshipping family of believers, you look to them and other Christians for encouragement and support. You may not always feel it.

You wonder how many more Sundays other worshippers will tolerate your squirmy two-year-old. You even wonder how many more Sundays *you* will tolerate her!

Take heart. None of us feels totally comfortable parenting in public. You wonder if your minute by minute parenting decisions are "right," especially if your child is the least bit strongwilled.

I have such vivid memories of Sunday worship with a squirmy two-year-old. After sixteen to eighteen months I usually began longing for a quiet, sedate child—or at least was tempted to wish away the next three or four years of squirmy Sundays!

We were fortunate, however, to be members of a parish whose pastor welcomed little children in worship. He didn't only *say* so. Young families also *felt* welcome.

One Sunday, after an especially active worship hour with our three young children, I must have looked exceptionally exhausted or overwhelmed. One of the deacons sought me out as we greeted friends outside on that sunny morning.

"I'm so glad I found you before you went home," he

said. "I just wanted you to know that I'm really happy to see you bring these three kids to church each Sunday. I know it's not easy to keep them all quiet and sitting still. You know, it really is okay if they make a little noise. That's how they learn, and worshipping is a part of learning. So keep it up!"

No one could have been more grateful than I was at that moment. I felt like a disheveled and exhausted mess. Yet there I was, getting encouragement from one of the *deacons*!

Deacon Doug will forever be on my list of great people. He sought me out just when I really needed to be encouraged. He made it possible for me to keep on doing what I felt was important. Sometimes I think about those "Shirley Sundays" from my own childhood and wonder if my mother had her own "Deacon Doug" to keep her going.

What my mother did have, which I didn't, was an extended family right around her to ease the load. When she needed help with her growing family, a cousin or aunt or grandparent was always nearby.

Available support, from people who also think these children are wonderful (remember—unconditional love?), is crucial for survival during the first three years of parenting. You can't do it all yourself is a hard lesson to learn. The bad news: SuperMom is a myth! And so is SuperDad.

They not only are myths; they are some of the most tenacious myths that have been around for decades, though the current labels are relatively new. The trap snaps so easily for all of us, making us think we really *can* do it all—and do it all *well* at that.

That's the time to remind yourself that you're human—read: *imperfect*. If we really could do it all—and do it perfectly—we wouldn't even need God. But the truth is we're well-meaning blunderers, and we do need God's forgiveness every day.

To get back to our topic, we simply need help now and then as we work at parenting. The challenge is to learn to accept help. Better yet, learn to ask for help and support. Now there's a tall order!

You can help yourself by expanding your understanding of "family." Yes, it means the two of you and your child (or children), but it also embraces a larger circle of relatives that support and love one another. The extended family draws on grandparents, aunts, uncles, cousins. But just as often it means a bond with other Christians who care about and support one another.

Extended family members who are physically close are particularly valuable if they can come to your aid as needed. But others are rarely more than a phone call or a postage stamp away. Work at keeping the communication lines open. That brings dividends: the support lines you need. Phone calls during the discounted hours are a good, inexpensive investment. You can alternate the calling between you and Grandma or Cousin Sally.

Reach out in meaningful ways to several members of your family tree. Remember that you are just a branch! Any branch that expects to stay green needs to tap into the trunk. The real trunk takes in your parents, aunts, uncles, but you can also tap into the other branches— your own brothers, sisters, and cousins.

A successful tap requires free flow of the sap of communication between the trunk and all its branches. The sap includes sharing family events. It also includes communicating feelings, worries, doubts, as well as the joys and victories.

Tapping the trunk but neglecting the source of food for it is, of course, foolish. The source of food is the Bible. Regular feeding on it is an absolute requisite during these busy years. Equally important is sharing the food with others on our tree to keep the sap flowing!

Each of us needs a tree nearby for maximum support. But not all of us are so blessed. Our tree may not be the supportive type. That's when we feel especially vulnerable, like a tiny, fragile seedling just getting its start.

But no tree needs to stand alone. Each of us can become part of a whole grove of trees. We can all get some support from the Christians around us—especially from the strong ones like Deacon Doug, from those in our community who worship at other parishes, both old and young, who are willing to give us support when we need it most.

If a grove of support is not easily identified, think about starting one of your own. Seek out the other young families in your church and in your community. Look for older adults whose children are grown. Find a senior couple or some singles and adopt them as close-by grandparents. They may need that relationship as much as you!

As with everything, we need to show good judgment. Take the child out of the church when the worship of others is obviously disturbed. Don't spank the child. Make church attendance a privilege, and talk to your child in that vein frequently during the week.

Remember when Jesus said, "Let the little children come to Me, and do not hinder them," He wasn't talking to their mothers. They were not the ones at fault. After all, they had brought the children. The ones getting (and needing) the scolding were the disciples, who were trying to keep the children from bothering Jesus. Jesus' directive was clearly the opposite. The disciples were to encourage the children to come. Likewise, the congregation and the child's baptism sponsors have the responsibility of bringing young children to Jesus. Obviously, that includes supporting and encouraging families with young children.

Children need to hear about Jesus. That begins in the home. But every home with young children needs support. Sometimes that support comes in the form of an encouraging word from a Deacon Doug. Sometimes it comes in the form of a neighborhood group that gets together, with children underfoot, to share frustrations, solutions, and joys. That group will be all the more supportive and helpful if it begins with the greatest source of power, the Word. A neighborhood Bible study group for young families can be a source of support as well as a way to reach out to non-Christians.

Another support is a Mother's Day Out program, in many communities run by church volunteers in church classrooms and basements. It is a limited form of drop-in child care for little ones, sometimes operating only one or two mornings a week. Mothers may drop off young children, together with diapers and food, leaving them with volunteers who will care for the children for two to three hours while Mom gets a much-needed break. Just the prospect of shopping *alone* for groceries sounds like heaven when you spend 98 percent of your time with an active toddler!

But church or community volunteers aren't the only ones who can give Mom a break. Every dad needs to be totally in charge of Tornado Tina for several hours a week while the other parent gets some respite (and vice versa!). Parenting is more than a full-time job. It's exhausting!

Exhaustion can be tolerated and even reduced if relieved by some regular time with an adult, or time to explore personal interests, read, or visit friends. Everyone needs time alone. Everyone needs time to refuel.

But you also need focused, nose-to-nose time with the newest member of your family. And while you are getting that special time with your child and building some new interests and routines, you are also giving your spouse a break.

Roots and Wings

Several years ago I came across a small plaque which made a lasting impression on me, probably because the combination of metaphors was a bit startling. It read, "Two things you need to give to your children. One is roots. The other, wings."

Although I didn't buy the plaque, I tucked the verse into my memory and have pulled it out every once in a while. Three years ago a series of events brought it up again.

I flew to Germany that summer to visit Lynelle, who had spent the year studying in Munich. My father gave me the names and birthplaces of my great, great grandparents, and their parents, and asked me to look for their towns while I was there. I wondered, "How will I ever find those little burgs that I've never even heard of?!" But I said, "Sure. I'll see what I can do."

So off I went, armed with a list of ancestors' names, a rented car, and a fuzzy memory of the German I had learned as a child. On my second day in Germany, I saw a sign along the Autobahn which announced, "Oberdachstetten, 1 Kilometer."

"Wow!" I thought (actually I was probably talking to myself at this point). "That's one of those towns I'm supposed to find!" So I made a quick exit off the Autobahn, no small feat in itself.

As I drove through the town, I had an incredible feeling of exhilaration, almost a soaring of spirit. I found an old man along the side of the road and, in my faltering German, told him what I wanted. "Are there any 'Klohas' still living here?" I asked, forgetting that he spoke no English! So we tried again. I managed to make myself understood and was able to learn that the only Klohas still in the area lived three towns away. The old man gave me the name and the directions to the town where Johann Kloha's father—my great, great, great grandfather—had been born. As I drove through the town, I promised myself that another day I would find those distant cousins and visit them, preferably on a day when my German-speaking daughter could come along. Now, driving through those streets, I gained a nostalgic sense of rootedness and belonging. This part of Germany with its villages seemed frozen in time for the past hundred years, and I clearly felt that, except for the single gas pump, almost nothing had changed since little Johann walked those streets as a child.

Two weeks later in Michigan, "home" for a family reunion, my father and I walked through the cemetery adjoining the picnic grove and the church that had been the scene of those "Shirley Sundays." He pointed out the graves of his parents and his grandparents, and then we found the grave of his great grandfather, the same Johann Kloha whose birthplace I had visited only two weeks earlier!

As I stood there with my back to the church, deciphering the time-weathered inscription, the sun cast a shadow of the steeple and its cross past the cemetery lawn. Just two weeks earlier I had made an eight-hour, non-stop flight in comparative luxury from Frankfurt to Chicago. What a contrast with the days and weeks that Johann and his young family must have taken to cover the same distance so long ago. "They did it for the cross," I thought. They came here to escape religious oppression in Germany (perhaps to become missionaries among the Indians in Michigan). They, too, were rooted in the cross.

How exhilarating, what a feeling of freedom, what a soaring of spirit to think that, because of who they were—my parents, grandparents, great grandparents and great, great Grandpa Johann—I now am rooted in Christ and can try my own wings to become the person God wants me to be!

Roots and wings. Both right there! Because of those roots of religious freedom I have wings to serve my Lord right now. I had almost forgotten about that little plaque I had seen several years earlier. But now it came rushing forward: "Two things parents need to give to their children. One is roots. The other, wings."

Roots and wings really can coexist! You're just starting to give them to your child. That's the task on which I've already spent a generation. But the idea didn't originate with that plaque. God wrote it into the Bible so many centuries ago!

Paul describes the Christians in Ephesus as "being rooted and grounded in love" (Eph. 3:17). Rooted in love, they would then be "able to know the love of Christ, which passeth knowledge" and be "filled with all the fullness of God" (Eph. 3:19).

Wings? Maybe. Isaiah used the metaphor: "They that wait on the Lord shall renew their strength; they shall mount up with wings like eagles, they shall walk and not faint" (Is. 40:31). In a sense, he used both metaphors. Waiting on the Lord assumes being rooted in God, I think.

As parents, your task is to do what my parents did

for me. First, make sure your children become rooted and grow in the Lord. Then let them try their wings. Don't push them out of the nest too soon. But also don't try to keep them when it's time to fly. Begin right now to let them test their own wings, little by little, under your watchful, encouraging eye, *right from the start.*